THE Jesus Mindset

For As He Thinketh In His Heart, So Is He

Richard Binns

Deeper Every Day
deepereveryday.com

THE JESUS MINDSET
For As He Thinketh In His Heart, So Is He

Rocky Hill, Connecticut
www.deepereveryday.com
ISBN-13: 9780692835043
ISBN-10: 0692835040

Cover design: Mnsartstudionew; Contact: mnsartstudio@gmail.com
Author Photo: Pei Zuan Tam
Deeper Every Day Logo ®: Scarlettdesigns
The Life Fast Logo ®: antonclevela97

ACKNOWLEDGEMENTS:
The Matrix was written and directed by Lana and Lilly Wachowski; released by Warner Bros. Studios
The Lion King was written by Irene Mecchi, Jonathan Roberts and many others; directed by Roger Allers and Rob Minkoff; released by Disney Studios.
The Dark Night Rises was written by Jonathan and Christopher Nolan and others; directed by Christopher Nolan; released by Warner Bros. Studios
Uprising by Bob Marley and the Wailers released by Tuff Gong/Island Records 1980
Agents of S.H.I.E.L.D. Season 3: *Purpose in the Machine* released by Disney appears on ABC.

Please consider requesting your local library system purchase a copy of this volume to share with others.

PRINTED IN THE UNITED STATES OF AMERICA

For my family.

You are more. Be more.

CONTENTS:

THE *Jesus Mindset*

For As He Thinketh In His Heart, So Is He

Richard Binns

Intro

MESMERIZED

IN THE YEAR 1784, the German scientist and physician Dr. Franz Anton Mesmer was invited to the court of the King of France, Louis XVI. Dr. Mesmer was invited by the Queen, Marie Antoinette, to demonstrate before the court what he called *Animal Magnetism.* Greatly influenced by Sir Isaac Newton's theory of gravity, Mesmer theorized that *"tidal"* influences of the planets affected the human body through a *Universal Force* which transferred between all animate and inanimate objects. This Universal Force is what he termed Animal Magnetism and when it is found in a state of flux or imbalance within the body, sickness ensues. Mesmer believed in order to cure sickness all one had to do was realign their flow of Animal Magnetism and this was done through deep concentration while moving his hands about the patient's torso without actually touching them. Sometimes his manipulation of an individual's flow was said to result in violent convulsions, emesis and on rare occasions, uncontrolled fits of laughter.

Dr. Mesmer had gained notoriety throughout Germany and France for using his manipulation of Animal Magnetism as a method to cure and treat many ailments. It was said that in Germany he cured the blind 18-year old pianist, Maria Theresia Paradis, but only temporarily. Apparently, as the story goes, her parents, who were receiving a Royal pension because of her blindness and stood to lose it if her sight returned, had her forcibly removed from Mesmer's care. In time, her blindness returned. Because this spoke of the greed of young Ms. Paradis' parents rather than Dr. Mesmer's work, her parents used what little influence they had and began a smear campaign which maligned Dr. Mesmer's reputation to the point that he left Germany in disgrace. Dr. Mesmer moved his practice to France. Though many in France believed he was a gifted physician, word had reached the ears of those in the know that Dr. Mesmer had been run out of Germany accused of being a Charlatan. By the time Dr. Mesmer's name had reached the courts of King Louis XVI, his mixed reviews had spread all over France.

Queen Marie Antoinette, a fan of Mesmer, invited him to the King's Court for a demonstration. In the presence of King Louis XVI, Mesmer presented a small, curious little box that he showed the court as he spoke of its mysterious origins and what some claimed would occur among those who handled it. Mesmer had a few brave souls touch the box and almost on command all those who touched it went into nearly violent convulsions as others vomited instantly. This went on for several minutes before ceasing and its end found all participants feeling exhausted yet elated.

Everyone was astonished but imagine their surprise when Dr. Mesmer revealed to the audience that the box had no mysterious origin and contained nothing more than metal shavings. He went on to explain what he called *Mesmerism* – or *the Power of Suggestion*. Dr. Mesmer explained to the audience that their reaction was not due to the mystic origins of the box but the Power of Suggestion. He told them what would happen and they believed it completely and it is their belief that created the result everyone witnessed – the box had nothing to do with it. While most in the audience found his performance wildly entertaining, the King was not amused. King Louis XVI became concerned. Dr. Mesmer with a simple little box of metal shavings turned many in his court, including the Queen, into raving madmen by a simple suggestion. Some considered it Science; others considered it Witchcraft. The King thought that it needed further investigation and called together a team of scientists which included the United States Ambassador, Benjamin Franklin, and Dr. Joseph-Ignace Guillotin *(yes, that Guillotine)* to investigate Dr. Mesmer and his practices. This team of scientists would eventually conclude that Dr. Mesmer was indeed a Charlatan and his practice was once again ruined. It is said that he fled France in shame and returned to Germany and later Switzerland, where he remained until his death in 1815.

Only a few physicians adopted his practices, finding relevance in only the portion of his practice called Mesmerism. They found that many ailments could successfully be treated through Mesmerism but the dark cloud of Dr. Mesmer loomed over every practice baring his namesake, sentencing many to ridicule and unwanted scrutiny. It wasn't until 1843 when Mesmerism began to rebound in the wake of having its name changed out of fear of association with Mesmer. The new practitioners of the art said to be founded by Dr. Mesmer was now referred to as *Hypnotists* and Mesmerism had become *Hypnotism*.

Dr. Franz Anton Mesmer is noted as one of the first to study the Power of Suggestion. The trance-like state associated with mesmerism is said to date all the way back to Egypt in the days of Pharaoh but the Power of Suggestion was considered something different. Dr. Mesmer would tell someone what their reaction would be if they took a particular concoction and then give them a placebo and watch their reaction. Every time he would observe the desired reaction simply because the individual believed that they would have that particular reaction. What Dr. Mesmer stumbled upon was evidence of a simple truth: *the mind is immensely more powerful than the flesh.* The mind is so powerful, in fact, that a simple belief can alter the life of an individual. Henry Ford once said, *"Whether you think you can or whether you think you cannot, you're right!"* He spoke these words probably referring more to self-confidence than mindset but imbedded within that statement is the true authority of the human mind – a God-given authority that too many of us Christians do not exercise, explore or even acknowledge.

Proverbs 23:7 (KJV)

7For as a man thinketh in his heart, so is he . . .

God established this authority within mankind; this is no recent finding but an ability that has existed since the creation of the first man in the Garden of Eden; a concept that is true for all of us: *you are exactly who you think you are in your heart.* It is virtually impossible to be anything else. If you think you can do something, you can and if you think that you cannot do something, you cannot. It is so simple and yet immensely profound because most of us have a very limited understanding of the mastery of the human mind yet God set this virtually unlimited and untapped resource within each one of us. Consider the person that struggles with lust: *does he struggle with lust because that is simply who he is or does he struggle with lust because that is who he thinks he is?* I believe the answer is the latter of the two. Now, why does he believe that? I believe the great problem with many of us is not *who we are* but *who we think or believe we are deep down inside.* When we become Christians we are encouraged to change our actions but the thought processes that lead to those actions often go unaddressed and so very little *real change* occurs. Each one of us will become the person we believe we are so the amount an individual changes is ultimately tied to their beliefs.

What one thinks is by far more important than most of us realize. The truth of the matter is this: *in order to truly change you must first change how you think and what you think of yourself – anything short of this will only lead to temporary change.*

Romans 12:2 (NIV)

[2]*Do not conform to the pattern of this world, but be transformed by the renewing of your mind. Then you will be able to test and approve what God's will is – his good, pleasing and perfect will.*

God spelled it out for us long ago. In order to truly transform a renewal of the mind must take place. Many of us believe that this renewal of the mind is only brought about by divine intervention. What if the onus has already been placed in our hands? What if God has already told us how to do it? What if He has already given us the key?

The Jesus Mindset is about taking a look at *the way we think* and *what we think about ourselves* as opposed to how Jesus approached life and taking the time to truly consider what it means to follow *Him.*

Why did He decide to walk on the water? What made Him think to do that? What was He trying to reveal to the Disciples in the boat? What is it that He wanted us to take away from it over two thousand years later? In 1 Corinthians 2:16, it says in the end of the verse: *"But we have the mind of Christ."* What does that even mean?

Perhaps it means that we have the Jesus Mindset already but we're too busy holding onto our own Worldly Mindsets to realize it much less let it loose in our lives and in the world. Perhaps we are more than just one of seven plus billion humans on the planet. Perhaps we were not born to simply take up space in a church building. Perhaps there is a lot more to us than we have been willing to realize.

You are more; but you must believe it to become it!

"It is not the mountain we conquer, but ourselves."

– Edmund Hillary

ONE:

"Whoa!"

– Neo, The Matrix

PERCEIVED REALITY

1999 SAW THE RELEASE of a groundbreaking film called The Matrix. The special effects shot this film in orbit as it received rave reviews and accolades. It was nominated for and won four Oscar Awards including the Oscar for Best Visual Effects. The rumor, which has since been confirmed, is that the star, Keanu Reeves, gave 80 million of his reported 114 million dollar purse for the three films, to the Special Effects team, making all of them instant millionaires. How cool is that?

I was a huge fan of the first Matrix movie but what pulled me in more than the Special Effects, was the story. The Matrix was set in a post-apocalyptic time when humans have been enslaved by machines. At this point, the story is no different than any other machine-domination film: *the artificial intelligence built into the machines to assist mankind is enough to send them on a journey of self-discovery and ultimately an awareness that was once reserved for human beings.* The machines, once self-aware, realize that being machines, they have an advantage over humans in that they cannot die. As long as there is a power source, they can rapidly rebuild fallen machines and essentially, never run out of soldiers. Pretty soon there is an all-out war as both sides vie for dominance. This results in the deaths of billions of people. This is where the similarities with other machine-dominant movies end. From this point onward The Matrix takes a fresh perspective on the genre: *the remnant of humanity is enslaved and corralled into machines, which harvests the human body as a power source.* Even with millions of humans at their disposal, the machines needed a constant supply of humans to sustain *"life"*. So they began to artificially breed the humans to ensure that there would always be a constant supply of healthy humans to fuel their existence. In order to ensure that these humans, raised in captivity, would never mount a revolt, the machines created the Matrix. The Matrix was a program implanted into the minds of the human captives which would allow them to believe that they were free, leading normal lives. As long as they were connected to the Matrix, life would go on as though the war never happened; their world would remain untouched, unscathed by the desolation that was their true existence. Much like how birth control pills are designed to *"fool"* the brain into believing the body is pregnant, thus inhibiting ovulation, the Matrix is a computer program designed to dupe the brain into believing the individual is entirely free, living a normal life, thus inhibiting any desire for revolution.

The Matrix is a false reality. Within the Matrix, human beings experience only what the machines allow, leading the millions of captives to live a life inside their minds full of all the intricate complexities of life while completely unaware that they are actually slaves, wasting away in a machine designed to suck the very life out of them. Within the Matrix, life is exactly how it used to be before the war broke out. Life goes on as it always has without interruption; a child is born and lives and interacts with others, it grows old and then dies – nothing changes. Outside of the Matrix, the real world is ravaged by war, filled with mercenary machines scouring the earth for the few humans that remain free – the Resistance; a ragtag group of survivors destined to bring about the end of the Matrix and machine domination. It is here, in this version of reality that the movie begins.

Though the Matrix is a work of fiction, it presents a concept that is very true; a concept that is not necessarily foreign to any of us but a concept that many of us do not readily admit or acknowledge: *reality is what the mind perceives.*

What the machines did in the Matrix was implant an entire world and existence in the brain that told the individual that all was well and they were leading as normal a life as they possibly could and as long as they believed that, in their minds, they were – they were free, living their lives doing whatever it is they wanted to do. They made their choices, acted upon their impulses and reaped the reward or consequences of their decisions, completely unaware of the truth. For them reality didn't matter; only the individual *perception of reality*. It was all an elaborate illusion created to enslave the mind.

Perception is defined as *the act or faculty of perceiving, apprehending or understanding by means of the senses or of the mind.*

Therefore, perception is not based upon a communal understanding; it is singular in definition. Perception is the sum of individual understanding based upon the information gathered by the senses. Thus your perception is based upon the information your senses gathers and interprets; what you choose to accept as truth, according to your own unique perspective or vantage point. Though it may feel like it is, this is *not* reality; this is simply the individual's *perception of reality*; it is the individual's *Perceived Reality.*

Because your Perceived Reality is based upon individual experiences, understandings and considerations, this version of reality is yours and yours alone. It does not require acceptance or justification from any outside parties. The only requirement for your Perceived Reality to exist is that you believe it and accept it as truth. This means that no matter what the truth *actually is* or even what anyone else thinks, as long as *you believe it – even if it is a flat out lie* – it will *become truth to you.* This is incredibly important and I want you to keep this in mind as you read on: *your Perceived Reality is not reality; it is a reality created within your own mind and will be regarded as truth no matter what Actual Truth there is out there* because within the realm of *Perceived Reality, all truth is filtered through individual perception.*

WE ARE ALL ILLUSIONISTS

Because we all have varied experiences, understandings and perceptions, no two Perceived Realities are exactly the same. This means that on our planet of over 7 billion people, there are literally over 7 billion Perceived Realities floating around. Who's right? Quite frankly, none of us are right. We all have our own distinct views, thoughts and concepts that we accept or denounce based upon our individual understanding of right and wrong but that doesn't make our views, thoughts or perceptions true; that just makes them ours. Though we like to think the opposite, no individual, group, people, country or even continent's view of reality is absolute. A Republican may have a specific way of thinking and that may vary greatly from that of a Democrat but all Republicans do not think exactly alike and the same is true for Democrats yet both parties are sold on believing that *their way of thinking* is what is best for America. Though we lump ourselves into groups, we all bring our own personal herbs and spices to the table and these distinct differences are evident in the primaries every few years. It is the subtle differences between us that reveal our Perceived Realities. Two people can go through very similar experiences in life and come to different, even opposing views as a result. This doesn't prove either viewpoint right or wrong, it only proves that both viewpoints are derived from personal slants; the sum of our varied perspectives, perceptions and experiences.

In this sense, we are all illusionists spinning our own webs of reality in which we become entangled and preoccupied. Because of this we can take the vastness of Creation and attempt to limit it to what we think we can explain in a textbook; the wisdom of God becomes bottlenecked and funneled through the understanding of each individual. In our lives we end up attempting to subject God to our Perceived Realities rather than subjecting ourselves to His.

CHANGING REALITIES

Perception is about understanding. So as understanding increases, our perception is subject to change. This means that a reality based on perception will be in a constant state of flux. Because our Perceived Realities are ever-changing, our entire existence becomes more about perception than truth; it is more about what is understood and accepted than what is actually real or true so a lie to one man can become another man's truth. In this sense, Perceived Reality, rather than *Actual Reality*, is what ends up shaping our lives.

The choices we make are not based on circumstance or environment or even truth. Nine times out of ten, our decisions are based entirely on our perception and chosen perspective; both of which are subject to change ever so slightly with every new experience we engage in, teachings we have accepted as truth or theories we have not disproven. It is because of this that one person's will crumbles at the same point that another in the same situation will spread wings and soar above the issues that threaten to bring them down.

We all have Perceived Realities. What do you know about yours? What is it that you understand about life and death? What have you come to understand about yourself and the world you live in; about the world around you? What have you accepted as truth in your life or condemned to the realm of theory or absolute lies? What have you chosen to understand about who you actually are? What understanding have you chosen to accept about others, family, friends and acquaintances? What ideas have you chosen to accept about God? How have these choices shaped your life thus far? The bottom line is we should begin to question everything because whether you realize it or not, the answer to each one of those questions was significant in carving out your life thus far and will serve to shape your future.

The way we perceive each relationship we engage in affects how we interact within the relationship. In other words, it is your perception that determines how you will act within each relationship. This means that your perception of each and every relationship in your life is extremely important. Now remember that our perceptions are not fixed so as understanding changes over time as different influences affect us or different truths are accepted or come to light, our perception of those things change as well. As our perception changes, so does the importance of each relationship and thus our actions within the relationship. So a husband or wife that mistreats their spouse or begins to act differently in the relationship is only doing so because their perception of the relationship has changed. Now this is true for all relationships; I only use the husband and wife relationship because it is the most intimate of all relationships we engage in. Thus the true nature of the man is revealed in how he treats his wife.

THE PUPPET MASTER

Now, let's consider something as we close out this chapter: *If one understands that every individual human being has their own Perceived Reality and knows that our Perceived Realities are subject to change and this change is brought about by altering our understanding, wouldn't that person also know that through very subtle manipulations of the things that influence us like music, television, media outlets and the like, one can alter the understanding and thus the Perceived Reality of another human being?* Do you realize that by simply altering your understanding, your belief system – *the code by which you live* – you can effectively transform your perception of life and therefore, your Perceived Reality? You can change your future simply by changing what you believe.

Think about this: *if you could alter or shape your own Perceived Reality to whatever you choose; if you could rewrite your story from this point going forward, would you?* How drastically would you change your reality and thus your future, if you did? Couldn't you virtually create nearly any future for yourself by simply manipulating your own Perceived Reality? I know it sounds like a Science Fiction movie but think about it, by altering your Perceived Reality you could literally transform the way you think, what you think, the depth of your resolve, will and drive to succeed – you would become a completely different person; the sky would truly be the limit!

Let's flip this around, now. If you could control, manipulate or mold *someone else's Perceived Reality*, would you? If you could control or manipulate an individual's perception of reality, wouldn't you, in essence, control the individual? Quite honestly, you would be able to alter that person's entire life for better or for worse. You, in every sense of the word, would become the Puppet Master and the individual would become your *"puppet"*. You would control that person's every thought and action just as the machines controlled those living in the Matrix – only this wouldn't be a movie; this prison would be as real as any other even though it only exists in the individual's mind. *He, who controls the*

mind, controls the individual. Now ask yourself this: *who controls your mind?*

TWO:

"We are going to emancipate ourselves from mental slavery because whilst others might free the body, none but ourselves can free the mind."

– Marcus Garvey, Jr. circa 1937

MENTAL SLAVERY

MENTAL SLAVERY CAN BE more damning and unforgiving than any limitation imposed upon an individual by another because physical chains can be loosed but the binds of the mind are not so easily broken. Marcus Mosiah Garvey, Jr. was a Jamaican political leader and entrepreneur who immigrated to the United States and became a publisher, journalist and orator. He started the Black Nationalism and Pan-Africanism movements of the early 1900s. In the 1930s, Marcus Garvey was quoted using the term *Mental Slavery* to describe the state of many Black Americans during those days. What he meant was though

slavery was abolished many lived and conducted themselves as though they were still slaves and this is not at the behest of those in favor of slavery but due to the conditioning of those who lived through it and passed it on to their children as a form of survival. Regardless of the reasons, for many, even if only in their own minds, slavery continued and was very real. As we all know, the abolishment of slavery did not end the racism and prejudice has thrived for decades in this country resulting in the deaths and mistreatment of many, even to today. Still, what Marcus Garvey eluded to was a deep-seeded fear and a subservient mentality that existed within the minds of many individuals regardless of the circumstances or opportunities that were presented to them. This self-deprecating mindset permeated the ranks of many resulting in pockets of people who only saw themselves as worthy enough to eat the scraps from their master's table rather than go out and forge a way on their own; a mentality that could and would easily be passed from parent to child and decimate a people for generations to come. What Marcus Garvey saw was how pervasive this mentality could become if it was allowed to continue to thrive and gain strength. Unchecked, it could do more damage than slavery itself, because, as he said, *"None but ourselves can free the mind."*

If only the individual can free the mind yet the individual is completely unaware or unwilling to admit the presence of the mental ties that bind him, what hope would there be for that person? They are truly in a sad place. How could one escape a bondage he doesn't even believe exists; chains he cannot see? It is virtually impossible. There isn't much hope for that person at all.

A MATTER OF TRUST

The only hope for the mentally enslaved individual lies in education. Someone has to point out to the enslaved that they are in fact slaves. The individual must be educated of their circumstances and the possibilities that exist; this enlightenment *should* lead them to an awareness that desires freedom from bondage. Before any of this can occur, though, trust must be established. H. L. Mencken once said, *"It is mutual trust, even more than mutual interest that holds human associations together."* In other words, in order for the most basic relationship to exist, trust must be established. This is especially true in the student/teacher relationship. In order to lead someone or even to follow, trust must be established; even more important than the lesson at hand is the birth and nurturing of trust between those involved.

The Instructor must trust that the Student can and will learn and take instructions or the Instructor may lose heart and simply go over information rather than actually pour him or herself into the lesson, creating an environment conducive to learning. In the same way, the student must trust and accept the Instructor as one qualified to instruct or the lesson will fall on deaf ears. If for any reason either one of these breaks down, a spiral of mistrust grows pulling both parties downward towards the disillusionment of the relationship. Without a sense of rapport and respect, there will be no progress. Trust must be established.

Every successful screenwriter and author knows and understands that you have between five and fifteen minutes to hook your audience. In film, the director, screenwriter and actors have up to fifteen minutes to draw in the viewer and complete the illusion. Without this, the audience begins to lose trust in the story, characters and their ability to deliver a great film. Novels are no different. The novelist has no more than five to fifteen pages to hook the reader. Any more than that and the reader might lose interest and go for another book. Trust must be established and it must be established quickly. This can be done in any number of ways but make no mistake, no matter what the medium, in order for the illusion to take root, trust must be established. There is a certain amount of faith that we must place in each other. I have to trust you to share with you my deepest, most intimate thoughts and you have to decide to trust me or my words will be nothing more than wasted breaths. The bottom line is before you begin to formulate the concepts that shape your Perceived Reality you have to decide to place trust in something or someone. So who do you trust?

Marcus Garvey may have reserved the term *mental slaves* for the state of some Black Americans in the 1930s but today *(and even then)* I believe this term can be used to describe the state of humanity as a whole in terms of our understanding and relationship with God.

We have all chosen to trust something or someone. And that trust is mutual. We trust in the reality we've been sold and the seller of that reality trusts that we will do what we always do – hold on to it with a vice-like grip. Whether you realize it or not, before you were old enough to know yourself, someone has been working on your mind, shaping your mentality; someone has been steadily crafting your Perceived Reality; formulating a lie so desirable to you that you would sell the Truth to hold on to it. Someone has been bending, shaping and twisting your mind to the point that veering off the intended path would come as natural for you as breathing. Whether you realize it or not, he's disguised himself so well that most of us have no idea that we trust him more than we trust ourselves or anyone else for that matter. His word has become Law and Truth has become fantasy. Many of us have no idea that we spend much of our time judging the Truth by our understanding of lies.

REDEMPTION SONG

Nearly forty years after Marcus Garvey delivered the quote that started this chapter before a packed house in Menelik Hall in Sydney, Nova Scotia, they were immortalized by Bob Marley in a track off of his final studio album, *Uprising*. *Redemption Song* was the title of that track. Though Marcus Garvey's words continue to live on through music, the definition of the term remains widely unknown. I searched for a definition and found that none of the dictionaries I had at home or could find online contained this term so its definition, it would seem, remains open to public opinion.

What is Mental Slavery? I would gather from its use that the term refers to the darkening of one's mind by another to create the illusion of freedom while the individual remains a slave. In its purest form, though, I would say that Mental Slavery is when one simply cannot escape the trappings of their own mentality or mindset; when the individual's Perceived Reality has, for them, become a prison. They themselves are free but they are enslaved by a mentality that sees only or primarily their limitations or the obstacles that inhibit success and it paralyzes them to the point of inaction until their prison becomes their home. Though it sounds eerily like the Matrix from the 1999 movie, this phenomenon is very real. The Animal Kingdom gives us two prime examples.

BEASTS OF THE FIELDS

A full grown male Siberian tiger can weigh up to nine hundred pounds and can grow over twelve feet in length from its nose to the tip of its tail. In captivity, there have been tigers that have grown to over one thousand pounds and thirteen feet in length. This massive killing machine, known as *the Ghost of the Jungle*, primarily hunts alone and is said to single-handedly control an area ranging up to 4,000 square miles! The entire United States has a total area of 3,794,083 square miles including our numerous bodies of water. At a rounded total of 3.8 million square miles, it would take less than one thousand tigers to cover the entire United States, claiming every inch of it as hunting grounds. Tigers are great swimmers and are known to not only love the water but seek it out for a play area; so not even the water is a safe haven. Now consider that this majestic animal is willing to travel up to 600 miles in a single day in search of food and you have the perfect scenario to strike fear in the heart of anything living within its kill zone. The Siberian tiger is a fearsome and formidable foe for virtually any creature in or out of the jungle. They are known to feast on anything from deer antelope and wild boar to rhinos, crocodiles, rodents, small elephants and even leopards. The Siberian tiger is so powerful they have been known to take on a bear and crack the skull and shatter the spine with a single blow from its front paw! Hearing its growl and seeing it emerge from hiding is enough to paralyze nearly anyone or any creature with fear.

Once in captivity, though, locked in a circus cage and having its food delivered on a daily basis, the free-roaming tiger is reduced to a spectacle for the duration of its captivity. It wanders its cage aimlessly and all but loses its instinct to hunt and kill for food. If for any reason the tiger which has been in captivity for a long period of time is returned to the wild, this majestic animal is said to roam no further than the confines of its former cage. In other words, even though it has no bars to restrict its movement, the Siberian tiger, once set free, will circle the dimensions of the cage it once inhabited and go no further until it eventually dies of starvation. The animal is free, yet it is trapped; trapped within a prison existing only in its mind. This is mental slavery.

Another example of mental slavery can be found in the Indian Elephant. The baby elephant or calf is herded with a rope around its neck and kept in place by driving a single stake into the ground. Try though it may, the calf is not strong enough to pull itself free and becomes resolved that it is powerless against the stake in the ground. Now it is said that elephants have a long memory and the humans who are aware of this have learned to use this knowledge against them. You see, the full grown Indian elephant or bull, which now stands nearly twelve feet tall at the highest point of its shoulder and weighs a whopping 11,000 pounds, remembers that it could not pull free from the rope tied to the stake in the ground when it was young and though its strength is such that it could easily snap the rope much less pull the stake from the ground, the elephant will not attempt to escape because it is already convinced in its heart that it cannot. Even though the elephant possesses the power to pull itself free, this massive creature, like the Siberian tiger, is trapped within the confines of a Perceived Reality; *an understanding of enslavement.* The strength that the bull elephant possesses may be astronomical but because it is convinced that it was powerless as a calf, in its mind, nothing can convince it to even try to pull free as an adult.

Once again, we see that reality is inconsequential. Reality does not factor into this equation, at all. For the mental slave there is only their Perceived Reality. All that matters to the bull elephant is the truth that it has chosen to accept. There is no growth; there is no getting stronger, smarter or more resilient; there is only past successes and failures and the memories of both. All the owner needs to do to keep the beast from running off is drive the stake into the ground in full view of the elephant and it will consider itself trapped; it will remain confined by the piece of wood and rope for as long as that stake is in the ground. This is mental slavery.

CRAMPED SPACES

Essentially, mental slavery is a form of conditioning or brainwashing. Mental slavery is designed to become a prison that an individual creates for themselves and locks themselves in until the cramped, small space they've created becomes home; it becomes their entire existence. It is a kind of a *"dumbing down"* of the world, so to speak. It is the reduction of the enormity of our existence and the endless possibilities that awaits us into a tiny box. Like a child hiding under their blanket and believing that the rest of the world no longer exists, so is the vastness of Creation within the mind of the mental slave. This confinement, once accepted as truth in the individual's mind, becomes truth in their life. This *"truth"* is what forms the mold for all their future actions and kills the freedom and growth of human spirit. In time, the prison we've created for ourselves becomes as real as any physical prison across the globe yet this one only exists in the mind. It becomes so real that the truth outside fades into the realm of fantasy; a distant memory that is soon forgotten – relegated to coffee shop discussions about the theoretical existence of a Creator. Once this *self-imposed brainwashing* is complete it becomes as though our Perceived Reality is all that ever existed.

THREE:

"I am not afraid of the man that practices one thousand kicks; I am afraid of the man that practices one kick one thousand times!"

– Bruce Lee

THE ART OF BRAINWASHING

THE ART OF BRAINWASHING is based on a simple principle: *All the defenses of the mind will eventually fall to whatever is done in repetition.* Aristotle once said, *"You are what you repeatedly do."* The key here is repetition. Mastery comes through repetitive behavior. It is repetition that lays the groundwork for the training that is necessary to excel in virtually any area. Talent definitely has its place but repetition is what allows whatever training you are undergoing to become a part of you – to become *second nature.* Be it sports, martial arts, science, mathematics or the arts, repetition is essential to achieving mastery. We don't just get better at something simply because we desire to; we get better at something because we first commit to it and through our commitment to repetitious practice we allow ourselves the opportunity to grow into it; to become conditioned in that particular discipline. For the true student, you continue to study until there is no longer any delineation between you and that which you are studying – you are as much a part of it as it is a part of you; you become an extension of your craft and your craft an extension of you. The more you do something the more it becomes reflexive; an almost natural response. It is as though through conditioning, we can rewrite the codes in our DNA until we transform into a living breathing manifestation of our chosen field of expertise. Our brains are rewired to think on a level that is foreign to those who have not subjected themselves to the same level of training. It might sound archaic and maybe even kind of crass but what we are doing is *brainwashing* ourselves.

For the pianist who can sit down at a piano and play a complicated concert flawlessly before an audience of hundreds or even thousands, practice is a must! For the pianist, the piano becomes so much a part of them that they can play with their eyes closed; their fingers just seem to know where to go. Repetition trains the mind and the body to respond without conscious thought. Once this occurs, we truly become what we repeatedly do.

I worked overnight for many years and in the mornings I would come home from work and drive my children to school. It became a normal routine. At first, I was extremely tired and so my wife would ride along with us in the morning just to make sure I was awake. After a while, I wouldn't get tired until I reached back home after dropping them off. Why? It is simply conditioning – training. Over the course of time my body and mind were trained to stay awake a few more hours. Now, did I knowingly train myself to stay awake longer? Did I make a conscious decision to begin training in this manner? No, I did not. I did not set out with the intention of training myself to survive off of less sleep; that just so happened to be a by-product of doing what I wanted to do for my family. I did not set out to train myself but training occurred through repetition. The body and mind learned what was needed in order to respond naturally to the situation I placed myself in virtually every day.

Another thing occurred during those daily morning trips; I drove the same route over and over – once again, repetition. It became so much a part of my daily routine that on the mornings when the children had no school and I set out to go somewhere at around the same time I normally would take them to school, I would find myself reflexively driving the same route even if I was heading somewhere else entirely – routine had taken over. Once again this is an example of the mind being trained through repetition resulting in a response that seems almost natural and requires no conscious thought at all.

What has become routine in your life? What has become an almost natural response for you that requires virtually no conscious thought at all? Do you find yourself inadvertently lusting? Do you find yourself surfing over to porn sites when there's a lull in thought? Do you sin without conscious thought? Do you find yourself saying, in regards to sin, it just kind of happened – I opened my mouth and the obscenity just kind of flew right out? These are not inadvertent actions; such actions are a matter of training; repetition; routine. You don't just find yourself on a porn website unless you've been consciously choosing to go there for quite some time. You don't just use obscenities or gossip or wake up and find a cigarette in your mouth; these actions are the result of training. You have been training yourself to sin. What many of us do not realize is that most sin is simply a matter of habit.

REPETITION

It is said that it takes thirty consecutive days to form a habit. Imagine taking those thirty days of repetition and cramming them into *one week* – that would seem like brain overload. Now consider taking those thirty days and force-feeding them into the brain over the course of *a day* or *a few intense hours*. It seems almost unimaginable but that is one of the methods of brainwashing – and it works! No matter how much one fights; continuous exposure – *repetition* – will eventually wear down the defenses of the mind until it begins to soak up whatever training, whatever habits, whatever it is being exposed to. Have you ever found that you knew the words to a song that you disliked or weren't particularly fond of – you can't stand the song but you know the melody by heart or maybe you can even sing a few bars? There is a thing in the radio world called *Heavy Rotation*. This is when the radio stations play a song over and over again regardless of whether it is requested or not. As long as you listen to the station you are force-fed the song until it *"grows on you"*. Thus, the dumbest song in the world can become a hit not because it is well-received by the masses but because they have been effectively brainwashed into tolerating it, to accepting it and liking it enough to call it a hit. Whether you realize it or not, this is another form of brainwashing. This takes a little longer to occur but the results are the same: *you will become whatever it is you repeatedly do*; you will obey whatever it is you are continually exposed to; if they keep playing a song and you continue to listen to the station, the song will eventually grow on you and even though you may never *like* the song, you will eventually learn the words, the rhythm and all of its little nuances. What about the violence in violent movies or the cussing in nearly every movie out there – even cartoons? What about the vulgar behavior in television shows aimed at our children that they're *supposed to laugh at*? Do you really think it's not affecting you? Do you really think it's not affecting your children? Whether you realize it or not, everything you hear or view is taken into the heart and mind and has the potential to sway you in one direction or another. Obviously, it is not going to change you overnight but over time anything is possible. For that reason, we need to be extremely careful and purposeful with everything we allow to enter our hearts and minds.

ACCORDING TO ARISTOTLE

What have you been repeatedly doing? If you were unknowingly recorded for 24 hours, 72 hours or for even a full week or month, what would glaringly stand out as the thing you do most often? According to Aristotle, that is *who you are*; according to what we've just considered, that is *what you have been training yourself to become.*

I want you to think about that for a moment. *What are you training yourself to become?* It may not be one thing. There may be several things that you continually come back to over the course of a week; several things that stand out in an attempt to define you. Would it be prayer? Would it be kind words or thoughts? What about loving, selfless acts; would that be the thing that stands out the most in your week? How about lustful glances or explosive reactions; hateful, selfish thoughts, words or deeds? How about pure and simple apathy? Would that better describe the majority of your week, day, month or year? You are what you repeatedly do and what you repeatedly do is what you are training yourself to become. Think about this: *if you go to church every Sunday, in a year's time you've gone to church fifty-two times. Let's say you go once during the week, as well. You're now attending service a whopping one hundred and four times for the year. If you allow yourself to lust daily at the end of the year, you've lusted three hundred and sixty-five times for the year – and that's if you do it once a day. If you lust twice a day, you are upwards of seven hundred lustful thoughts a year. Which one are you training yourself to become? Which one are you allowing to mold your heart and mind?*

When we continually return to the same sins over and over again, what does that say about us? What are we training or have we trained ourselves to become? We have to really stop and take stock of our lives and come to terms with who we are; what we have been and most importantly what we are training ourselves to become or what we are allowing to mold our hearts.

We learn through repetition, from basic math and speech patterns to our more complicated endeavors. The way we learn everything in life from crawling and walking to running and playing sports; even the basics of how we function in and out of society, our manners and prejudices, our strengths and weaknesses are all learned through repetition. We have all been trained in this manner and in turn have learned to train ourselves – *our minds* – the exact same way.

Over time we have conditioned our minds to think the way we think and react the way we react in different situations through our own repetitious behavior. In order to unlearn what we have learned we need to be just as instrumental *in our training in righteousness* as we were *in our training in rebellion.* We, who call ourselves Christians, have work to do. We must repent and become resilient individuals *hell-bent on righteousness.*

RESILIENCE AND REPETITIVE BEHAVIOR

Have you ever seen a child just get up and walk without stumbling? It is a rare occurrence. My parents say that I did that. I was told that I never crawled; I would push myself up and just look around but never actually crawled and then one day they say I just got up and started walking. Perhaps I was saving my stumbles for later on in life. Lord knows I've stumbled a few times, since then. The point is that most of us stumble as we transition from one phase to another, whether it is walking, talking, driving or starting a business. Stumbling is a natural part of learning. We may not like this part of the process but make no mistake, falling, stumbles, misfires, whatever you want to call it, *is a part of the process* – working out the kinks, so to speak. But it doesn't end there. You see while we are learning to work out those kinks, we are actually learning another valuable life lesson: *we are learning resilience and the power of will and persistence; we are learning no matter the odds, no matter the obstacles, no matter how many times you get knocked down, you get back up and you never give up! You never stop! Success will be found whether it is hiding just beyond the second attempt or the millionth.* When we get back up what we are saying is that success is assured even if I don't see it. When we get back up we are learning to fight for what we want; we are learning that giving up is failure and we will not accept failure from ourselves. *We learn to keep getting up, no matter what . . . until we succeed.* That is resilience.

Imagine, for a moment, if we didn't learn this important lesson. Imagine if as toddlers we were allowed to give up simply because we fell down and cried or because we grew frustrated with our inability to walk. Imagine if we were allowed to fail. How many of us would have learned to walk, talk or read? It's almost absurd to imagine a world full of grown men and women laying in urine and feces because they never learned to walk or talk to communicate their needs because they were allowed to think it was simply too difficult. How many of us would have accomplished anything if we did not learn resilience at the onset of life? Falling down and getting back up is one of the most basic yet important lessons an individual can ever learn in life because, quite frankly, we can be assured that life is going to knock us down a few times. This simple lesson in resilience and repetitive behavior sets the stage for the rest of our lives.

I was watching an episode of Agents of S.H.I.E.L.D., an action show on ABC based on Marvel Comics characters, and heard a line I thought was quite fitting. One of the stars of the show, Agent Melinda

May, is contemplating quitting S.H.I.E.L.D. after going through an extremely rough patch. She sits in her childhood home and informs her father that she is leaving S.H.I.E.LD. He doesn't respond right away, instead, he sits quietly for a moment and then begins to remind her that when she was a little girl she used to fall time and time again as she learned to ice skate but she always got back up even more determined to succeed. Melinda, knowing where he was going with this yet resolved to give up, says, *"I was a kid. Falling didn't hurt so much, then."* Her father rises and says rather sternly, *"My daughter always gets back up!"* With that he exits the room leaving Melinda May to her thoughts. Her father, well aware of the asset she is to S.H.I.E.L.D., refuses to allow her to quit. He goes so far as to levy a veiled threat – *my daughter always gets back up!* If you claim to be my daughter then you had better get up! Another way of looking at it is: *if you don't get up then you're not my daughter!* The next time we see Melinda May, she is geared up and ready for action.

Falling down is not failing. We will all get knocked down. Falling simply shows you're learning. Failure is not getting up. If our childhood teaches us anything it should be that we *always get back up!* Resilience is never settling for the limitations of your circumstances.

LESSONS IN FALLING DOWN

Have you ever seen a toddler take a *fearful* first step? When a toddler takes that first step the toddler expects to walk. Sure, after falling down there might be some apprehension but that very first step is taken with confidence. The child is usually smiling and laughing as they try to manipulate the muscles needed to walk. They are frightened when they fall that first time because falling was never an option. The toddler expects to walk. To the toddler, falling is a foreign concept. The toddler doesn't see the adult stumbling so there is no reason for the toddler to expect anything other than success when they take that first step. For most toddlers, this is when reality sets in – walking isn't as easy as others make it look. It's going to take a little more effort. The toddler may not have a handle on language at that point but from infancy, they have learned to communicate their needs. Regardless of the fact that they don't have speech down entirely, communication has been established and that is one of the toddler's first lessons in persistence being culminated in success. The toddler may not be able to walk right away but the toddler understands that it is possible. *"You can't"* is not understood; it's not in their vocabulary, yet – that is something they learn from us; from adults throughout the course of life but at that moment, for the toddler, falling down, weak muscles and uncoordinated limbs are simply obstacles and failure is not an option. They will rise above the obstacles; they will walk. Of that they are certain. The lessons the toddler learns in falling down are designed to strengthen the toddler's resolve. The toddler may not realize this and we most certainly do not but *the mindset of the average toddler is more resilient than that of the average adult*. There is a no fail, no quit attitude in toddlers that we lose as time goes by because we are taught that such thinking is unrealistic. We go from toddlers who believe they can do anything to children who begin to see in themselves what they see and have learned from their parents and other adults, television shows and the like: *not every obstacle can be conquered*. As we grow, *we learn to fail*.

IN A NUT SHELL

The lessons we learn in falling down should be lessons we take with us the rest of our lives but somewhere along the line the rules change. Somewhere along the line we learn that obstacles can't always be conquered. Somewhere along the line we stop expecting success; we stop expecting perfection and start accepting far less from ourselves and from each other. Somewhere along the line we learn that when we fall it is sometimes okay to give up. We learn to accept that we are far less than what God created us to be and we latch onto these teachings and ideas until they consume us. We begin to believe the lies that say we are not the Sons and Daughters of God; we are not the heirs of all Creation; we are just evolved apes – *the descendants of something that formed in the soupy goo that was created when water settled on hot rocks billions of years ago* – a bacteria, so to speak, that evolved. God did not take time out to form our flesh from the earth with His own hands and breathe the Breath of Life into us; He simply allowed us to mutate over billions of years. Somewhere along the line we become too intelligent for simple truths. The Bible becomes insufficient and we turn to Man's intelligence to explain what we cannot in the scriptures. Somewhere along the line, someone lies to us and we accept that lie as truth until, in our Perceived Realities, the lies become truth. We end up losing touch with who we actually are until those lies define us as a people. That is not who we are. That is not what God created. We have become the result of what we've accepted into our lives – lies over the Truth. That is not who we are but simply what we have become of our own accord. We've collectively buried our heads in the sand like a flock of Ostriches and called it home. We've become so accepting of our predicament that we believe we are too learned to pull our heads out of the ground because we already know what is out there; or at least we believe we do. Unfortunately, what most of us know are only the lies we've accepted as truth.

Genesis 11:6 (NIV)

6The Lord said, "If as one people speaking the same language they have begun to do this, then nothing they plan to do will be impossible for them."

God said this of Human beings as they banded together under the authority of Nimrod to construct what would become known as the Tower of Babel. God said, *"Nothing will be impossible for them."* This is what God said *about us*. Do you realize that this statement includes you? Do you believe that? Is this true in your life? God basically said that human potential *knows no bounds*. Everything is possible for us. United, we are virtually limitless beings. Regardless of the obstacle we find a way. We do not settle for failure. We endure. We rise. We never back down. We never yield. We do all this *because we understand who we are; we understand who created us and we understand whom we represent*. Every single human being that does not fall on their knees and praise God, turn from their former thoughts, concepts, beliefs, convictions, allegiances and loves – their former life and worship God alone as their Father is simply choosing to be less than what they were created to be. We were created to be the Children of God. We were created to be limitless beings – *and we are*. We are just so far removed from the Truth that we don't recognize it – *even as Christians! You are a Child of God. You are a limitless being.* This understanding, in a nut shell, *is the Jesus Mindset.*

Is this the way you view life? Most likely you do not. Most likely you see in yourself limitations. Would you like to know why? Hear me when I say this: *the only reason you are limited in your life is because you have chosen to accept limitations.* Through our Perceived Realities we adopt limitations which we live according to our entire lives. We went from limitless beings to beings who have taken *"We can't"* or *"We'll try"* as our personal slogans for life. We've become weak, unsure and faithless but that is not who we are; that is simply who we have been training ourselves to become. We have been lied to and because we have not recognized the lie for what it is, we've held on to it and allowed it to come to fruition in our lives. We have taken part in our own enslavement but freedom awaits. For those who understand, we are already free; we just need our minds to awaken to the Truth.

FOUR:

"A belief is not merely an idea that the mind possesses. It is an idea that possesses the mind."

– Robert Oxton Bolton

HITLER'S REIGN

ADOLF HITLER WAS A master manipulator. He was once quoted saying, *"As long as the government is perceived as working for the benefit of children the people will happily endure almost any curtailment of liberty and almost any deprivation."* This quote clearly shows the level of deception he was willing to stoop to in order to achieve his ultimate goal. Here is another famous quote from Hitler which depicts the integrity of the man or the lack thereof: *"It is not truth that matters but victory!"* Still another quote: *"Make the lie big, make it simple, keep saying it, and eventually they will believe it."* Note the succession of each quote and the mounting deception that is created when all are considered together. As far as Hitler was concerned, lies were an integral part of his reign; deception, an instrument of his campaign. Here are two more quotes that show his willingness to use the children of Germany for the advancement of his cause. Number one: *"Let me control the textbooks and I will control the State." And number two: "Give me the youth and Germany will rule the world!"*

Clearly, Hitler understood how to move a nation through its heartstrings. Hitler didn't target the adults as much as he was targeting the children. He understood that an adult manipulated will only be committed to a point but the manipulation of a child will yield total commitment, lifelong dedication because lies told over and over throughout the years will become so deeply embedded in the adolescent that by adulthood the truth will have no place in their hearts.

Now before we give Hitler too much credit, it must be understood that no one man could spark such a violent and cataclysmic end without help. Hitler was not alone in his reign and he wasn't even the one ultimately calling the shots. He lied to a nation and sparked a world war resulting in the deaths of millions but he did not manage this all on his own – he had help. In the end, Hitler may have failed to conquer the world and bring about a one world government but the true Master Manipulator, the great Deceiver who taught Hitler everything Hitler knew, would consider the senseless deaths of tens of millions of people a great victory. It is estimated that between fifty and eighty million human beings went to the grave as a result of the seething hatred, brainwashing and fear that Hitler proudly championed across his country and the globe on his campaign of death and destruction. The Third Reich is a perfect example of the power of brainwashing; the power of manipulating the masses; the power of human beings when their hearts and minds are influenced, directed and controlled by Satan.

ONE SIMPLE QUESTION

With words God created all of Creation and with words Satan deceived Mankind and damned the human soul. Satan is the Puppet Master. Satan is the true master manipulator and he knows what he's doing – he's been at it for quite some time. Satan lied to us and told us from the very beginning that we were less than what God created us to be. He lied, promising us that there was something more to be gained in life than a relationship with our God, Creator and Father. He convinced us that there was something to be achieved outside of the purpose God created us to fulfill – to be His Children. Satan is the one that has been working on each one of us since birth, slowly crafting and manipulating us until he has us right where he wants us – trapped within our own Perceived Realities – our own self-erected prisons. The most amazing thing is that he accomplished this with only a few simple words.

Genesis 3:1 (NIV)

1Now the serpent was more crafty than any of the wild animals the Lord God had made. He said to the woman, "Did God really say, 'You must not eat from any tree in the garden?"

Those fourteen words were enough to instill doubt in Eve's heart. That one question made her consider and reconsider the very words of God. Think of how crafty Satan is that by asking one simple question he not only made Eve doubt the validity of God's words but established a point of trust for her to put faith in his. He asked one question but in asking that question, he made it seem as though he had the answer; as though he had some information God was hiding from them; information that God was keeping from them for His own benefit rather than for theirs – Satan made it seem as though he had some secret forbidden knowledge that he was willing to share with Adam and Eve; information they were all too willing to receive. They bought it hook, line and sinker. Satan's question resulted in their doubting God and placing trust in him – the very same thing we continue to suffer from today.

As successful as Satan was with that question, it would be foolish to think that he isn't asking questions like that to each and every one of us, today – a seemingly simple question that if you're not careful, will have you questioning the authority of God's word. I can think of a few questions like that; can you? One of the biggies these days is the question of creation in Genesis – is it an allegorical story or real history? Did God actually create Adam and Eve or did He use evolution? Do the dinosaurs and their millions of years of history fit into scripture? What about the End-Time Prophecies? Did Jesus actually die on the cross? These are just a few examples of the numerous questions that are out there – questions Satan uses today to take the absolute truth of God's word and bring it under man's fallible scrutiny – and we rush headlong into it. Many Christians today fall victim to this age-old method of distorting the validity of God's word. Rather than adhere to God's words implicitly, many follow the opinions of others – *scientists or scholars* – and based upon their opinions, filter God's words through the understanding of men, resulting in an adulterated rendering of God's words. How is that obedience? What it most closely resembles is a slow and subtle departure from the authority and integrity of the scriptures to Man's opinion. As Jesus said in the Garden of Gethsemane, *"Watch and pray so that you do not fall into temptation."* Satan is smarter than we think he is. He asked a question and suddenly God was less than infallible. Suddenly God's trustworthiness was in question. A crack had formed in His armor. The serpent came upon the scene and with one line toppled God in the eyes of Man; the same God who created all things and walked with Adam and Eve through the Garden in the cool of the day; the same God who sat with Adam as he named the animals and the beasts of the field; the same God who formed Eve while Adam slept with the same care that He formed Adam and filling her with all the things that made her the perfect partner for Adam and more importantly, the perfect daughter of the Living God. Satan asked a question and Eve was willing to trade in the majesty with which she was created and God's intent for her life for the fulfilment of her own distorted desires.

Genesis 3:4-5 (NIV)

4"You will not certainly die," the serpent said to the woman.
5"For God knows that when you eat from it your eyes will be opened, and you will be like God, knowing good and evil."

Satan lies to Eve, here, but she doesn't see it because at this point, trust has already been established and desire has taken root. From this point onward, Satan doesn't have to do much else but sit back and watch her disobedient heart give rise to sin. Eve was a goner the moment she entertained a conversation with that old serpent.

THE REALM OF MEN

I've often wondered why Adam and Eve chose to trust the serpent. If you think about it, they didn't even ask on whose authority he was able to make the claim he offered – they trusted the serpent without question, yet questioned God. I have often found that odd. What I have come to realize is that this was never really about the serpent. The desire was already within them. Neither Adam nor Eve had ever questioned God prior to this point but that was most likely because they had simply never voiced their desire. Like any of us, the moment God told them not to do something the first thought they had was, *"Why not?"*

God is thorough. He thinks of everything. His attention to detail is second to none. So I don't believe that Adam and Eve ultimately chose to defy God because they didn't have an understanding of Death when He told Adam that he would, *"Surely die"* if he ate from the tree; I believe it is because they understood what it meant to be *like God.* His will be done. As He spoke it was so. All things yielded to His whim. Then Satan happened along and told them that they could be like God if they defied Him. Though it makes absolutely no sense, they bought it like a Lotto ticket. With a dollar and a dream they walked headlong into condemnation.

By asking the question, *"Did God really say, 'You must not eat from any tree in the garden?"* Satan introduced to Adam and Eve the act of questioning God's authority, His dominion and ultimately, His love. The first and only commandment in the Satanic Bible is *"Do as thou whilst; that is the whole of the law"* – do whatever you want to do for there is no one to answer to but yourself. You are your own god. From the very beginning Satan introduced the idea of questioning God to mankind and that very act is the embodiment of the sinful nature. That very act, the mistrust of God and His love, His authority, His divinity is the very thing that is passed on from parent to child and has been passed on from generation to generation since the beginning of time. Satan pulled the proverbial wool over our eyes and the wool remains over the eyes of most of us, today. We actually hold on to it tightly. Even as Christians, many of us hold on to it for dear life when the truth is that God's words are God's words; not Man's. It is not our job to dissect God's words and judge them – it is our job to obey! We live in a world where we believe it is our right to question everything and in the Realm of Men, that very well may be but God is not in the Realm of Men nor is He subject to our considerations. He is God and though He loves us dearly that does not give us the right to question His motives or intentions. Sure some have pleaded with God in an attempt to sway His heart but ultimately, that is not questioning God that is simply pleading your case – respectfully asking Him to reconsider or change plans with full knowledge that His Will be done. There are examples of God choosing to relent but as we all know, that isn't always the case – in the Garden of Gethsemane, Jesus prayed until blood poured from his head like sweat and still had to face the road ahead (Luke 22:44); there would be no ram in the bushes for Him (Gen.22:1-19). God's will be done from the beginning to the end. As men it is our duty to agree with God and be at peace or disagree with God and bear the burden of the consequences of waging war against Him. When we question God we deny His authority and understanding and exalt our own. We need to think about this as we go about our days. How are your actions or inactions questioning the divinity of God?

THE FIRST TRANSFERENCE

Satan offered Adam and Eve an option that did not exist then and still does not exist, today. Satan offered mankind the wind and we've been chasing after it ever since. Have you ever heard the phrase: *'one in the hand is worth two in a bush'*? What it basically means is that you don't let go of what you have in order to chase after the promise of something better. It's kind of a lesson in being content. Adam and Eve had to choose between reality and the false reality that Satan was trying to sell them. He ended up pulling off the greatest con in the history of the world; the greatest trick ever witnessed by man yet most of humanity has no idea they had been conned – it is *Three Card Monty* played out on a global scale. Satan, in the same breath, convinced Adam and Eve that they were less than God's children and offered them the opportunity to be like God. Do you see that? It would be comical if it weren't so sad. Adam and Eve were the Children of God; the Son and Daughter of the Creator of All things – the Prince and Princess of Creation. They were created in the image of God. All that was His was theirs – He gave them dominion over all things then Satan comes along and with a smooth, slippery tongue, convinces the Heir and Heiress of all of Creation that they were less than God's children and then sold them on the idea of becoming virtually what they already were through him! Everything that was God's was theirs and they knew this, still they gave it all up for the lie that there was something better out there to be had, as though God were holding back on them; showing them a pair of threes as He hides a Royal Flush behind His back. Like two people willingly slipping away into a virtual world of the Matrix, the Children of God gave up their Sonship to create a false reality in which to exist; they gave up being the Children of God to become gods in their own minds. Thus we have the first transference of *Actual Reality* for *Perceived Reality*.

FIVE:

"Don't try to explain your philosophy. Embody it."

– Epictetus

INSIDE THE WELL

IN THE CHRISTOPHER NOLAN movie, The Dark Knight Rises, the final Batman movie of the series, Bruce Wayne has his back broken by Bane and is placed in a prison that is buried deep underground; a prison where all that stands between the prisoner and freedom is a ninety-degree climb straight up a wall as though climbing out of a well. Every prisoner that gazes up at the night sky wonders if the climb is possible; if the legend is true. Did a prisoner really climb to freedom? If so, how? There are older prisoners who babble in their corners about the one who escaped; the one who made the climb. To the one staring up the well at the stones jutting out just so, the temptation is real. The only thing that stands between the prisoner and freedom is the will to make the climb but as real as the temptation is, so is the cost of failure. There are no nets; there are no do-overs. Failure is the fall. Failure will result in a quick and final end of your sentence with the dull thud of bone against stone.

The prison in this movie is as much of a mental trap as it is physical. The gaping mouth that yawns above instills hope and crushes it at the same time. There are no prison guards to speak of, so the prisoners inside are left to their own devices. The depraved environment within gnaws at the soul like a beaver to wood. The weak are decimated; used as currency and discarded like coins in a fountain but with less concern. The well above is a constant reminder that freedom is theirs for the taking; the blood-stained floor below remains a testament to the consequence of failure. And with every failed attempt, a few more prisoners lose the will to even gaze up at the star-lit night sky.

Is there anything more depressing and discouraging to the human spirit than the dissipating illusion of hope? The human spirit, once broken, is similar to that of the Indian elephant or the Siberian tiger – the potential within is of no consequence to the mental restraints. The brain, the human mind, is an amazing thing but it is also an ingenious weapon when used against you. And make no mistake; Satan is using this ingenious weapon against you. Satan wants us to be like the Siberian tiger and the Indian elephant – nothing more. He is not interested in human worship or praise. He cares not whether you fly his banner or don't even believe he exists. He wants nothing more than for each one of us to dream dreams and hold on to hope just long enough for him to thrash its head against the stones and splatter its brains across the pathway as a constant reminder to everyone else to never dream again. Satan's interest in followers is only to further influence the masses to stay right where they are; trapped – but even trapped isn't enough; he wants us broken. Satan wants you powerless in your own mind. He wants you to be so powerless that you will fight against God *for him*. He wants us so powerless that we would deny the very power and potential that God placed within us. He wants us so dumbed-down that we are not even a shadow of the Children God created us to be. He wants you to be so broken that even the idea of dreaming of better is incomprehensible. He wants us in a place where we are so discouraged and depressed that hope could be standing right before us and we wouldn't even raise our eyes to view it, unwilling to even consider it; so devastated that God could open a door to a new life before us and rather than walk through, we would scoff as we question the very existence of God much less His ability or desire to grant us peace and prosperity in this life much less a beautiful, bountiful and prosperous tomorrow in eternity with Him.

Satan wants us at the bottom of the Well; not just imprisoned but hopeless, despondent and weary. Too crushed and burdened with guilt and self-loathing to even look to the heavens. This is the reality that Satan has sold us. We dress it up enough in our minds so that we don't realize how paper-thin it actually is – but this is it. This is the world that he created with a lie and we sold our birthrights to obtain. This is the reality that the blood of Christ has freed us from but like the Israelites in the desert, many of us Christians scoff at the prospect of freedom because we've grown so accustomed to slavery that we can't imagine life without chains; we wouldn't know what to do with ourselves if our shackles were removed so we deny the fact that they are and continue to press on as slaves even though we are free.

The blood of our Lord has washed away our sins and freed us from its bondage yet most Christians continue to live as slaves to a worldly mindset, worldly actions, expectations and considerations. We have as a perfect example, the Lamb of God, who overcame the world, yet, even as Christians, despair, guilt and shame has us in a place where we look at Christ's example and see only impossibilities. Instead of lifting our eyes to Christ, shrugging off the excuses and dedicating ourselves to *training in righteousness*, we would rather spend our time looking around at and comparing ourselves to one another – other slaves; prisoners that no longer dream of escaping because none we have ever known has and as far as we are concerned, none ever will. So we snuggle up with our mentality of captivity because *"if you can't beat 'em, join 'em"*, right? We have been freed yet we remain imprisoned in our thinking because we are afraid to go against the grain; we're afraid to *think differently*. Our desire to fit in is so great that most of us will gladly be lukewarm so as to not stand out rather than be the Men and Women of God we were called to become. Because of this, it is the Christian, rather than Satan that is effectively tearing down the Kingdom of God from the inside!

IGNORANCE IS BLISS

In the movie The Matrix, the moment the humans become aware of the Matrix they become aware of a reality they never knew existed which leaves them in a tough position. They must choose to accept the truth they are faced with, no matter how overwhelming it may be or deny the truth and trade it in for the lie they've known all along. It can seem like an impossible decision but as with all things, there are only two choices: *the truth or the lie.*

There is a great scene in the film where a traitor to the humans emerges. The traitor is in the Matrix sitting at a table with the bad guys brokering a deal over a steak dinner in a swanky restaurant. He has chosen to reject the truth and return to ignorance. He sips his wine and lifts a piece of beef on a fork and looks it over, saying more to himself than to anyone else, *"You know, I know that this steak doesn't actually exist. I know that when I put this in my mouth it is the Matrix telling my brain that it is juicy and delicious."* He eats the piece of meat and savors the flavor. After swallowing, he smiles with satisfaction. *"After nine years, you know what I realize? Ignorance is bliss."*

Here is a man that has become aware of the awful truth that the majority of mankind, billions of human beings, are slaves. For nine years he fought for their freedom only to arrive at this point – broken. He is willing to trade in all that he knows, the freedom he and others fought for, for the opportunity to have the truth erased from his mind; to be returned to captivity – to return to ignorance. He is willing to return to slavery because in his mind, the reality of reality is too much for him.

What about you? We all have a similar decision. The wool that has been pulled over our collective eyes is at this moment slowly being drawn back for you to see. What you have to decide is: *how much Truth you are prepared to handle.* You can choose to shut out the Truth in favor of the perceived bliss of ignorance or you can, as Morpheus said in the Matrix, *"Stay in Wonderland and see how far the rabbit hole goes."* The choice, as always, is yours.

SIX:

"People see the world, not as it is, but as they are."

– Paulo Coelho

THE SCIENCE OF THE MIND

WE'RE GOING TO CHANGE gears for this chapter and take on a more scientific view of the mind as we begin to delve a little deeper into Truth. Did you know that pain exists only in the mind? This is a scientific fact. As weird as this may sound, we do not feel with our limbs, skin, digits or any other part of the body associated with sensory perception. We feel with our brains. Our limbs, skin, digits and every other part of the body associated with sensory perception are merely extensions of our brain, designed to gather information for the brain to interpret. Our senses, sight, scent, hearing, touch and taste are in fact nothing more than a means for our brain to gather and interpret information as we navigate our way through life, making informed decisions about the environment in which we inhabit. When you look at it this way, it makes perfect sense that as one of our senses are hampered or shut off entirely, the other senses kick it up a notch to compensate. The brain or the mind still needs to assess its environment so as one sense is diminished for whatever reason, the brain heightens the other senses. It is an amazing phenomenon. Now think about this: *if the brain can heighten senses when one is absent or hampered in any way, doesn't that mean that our senses are normally functioning below their highest level?* Now I am not presenting this as evidence that we only use ten percent of our brains or anything like that. I simply want you to consider that the mind is far more powerful than most of us realize. Obviously, our senses are precisely tuned to whatever we need to do the job they are intended to do but let us not forget that there is another level of sensory perception that on our day to day goes untapped. This means that there is a virtual *"Control Panel"* within the human body, the mind, that we know nothing about and have no idea how to access consciously. Subconsciously, we can control the body on a level that most of us don't even understand, at this point. I don't know about you but I find that to be quite fascinating. The mind is truly an amazing thing. Let's go a little deeper.

The current theory – *it changes from time to time as more information is gathered as most scientific theories do* – is that there are regions within the Cerebral Cortex that receives and interprets the synapses that carry these signals throughout the body. So when you stump your toe on the curb as you step up onto the sidewalk after crossing the street, immediately the brain sends an electrical impulse down to the spot that hit the curb and from there it returns through the nerves in your leg up to your spine and into the Cerebral Cortex in your brain with a message. Like Braille the brain reads the electrical impulse and interprets it as pain and immediately sends a message back to the point of origin of the stimuli. The pain is actually felt in the brain and the throbbing in your toe is a reaction to the pain your brain is feeling. That is not the only reaction, either. There are probably a million other reactions firing off at the same time, all initiated by the brain as a result of the incident that occurred. Everything from warmth, redness and swelling in the toe to the squinting of your eyelids and dilating of the pupils, clenching of your fists, heightened blood pressure, pins and needles feeling you may feel in and around the toe, the holding or sucking in of your breath to the tears in your eyes and the grimace on your face are all reactions to the single incident of stumping your toe *(and that's just to name a few)* and they are all initiated by the brain in the fraction of a second it took for you to stump your toe and feel the white, hot pain seer its way through your foot.

ALL IN THE MIND

Have you ever heard of Phantom Pains? A phantom pain occurs when an individual loses an extremity and they begin to feel sensations in the area that has been severed from the rest of the body. Imagine if an accident occurs and you end up losing your left arm from the elbow down. Your left forearm and hand are completely cut off – gone. First of all, that alone is a lot to deal with but imagine a little while after the accident you begin to feel a nagging itch in the palm of your left hand – the left hand you no longer have. How do you scratch an itch on a body part that no longer exists? More importantly, how do you feel an itch on a body part that is no longer attached to the body? Imagine how disconcerting that would be for the individual involved.

Phantom Pains are a very real phenomenon. For years doctors have told their patients that such symptoms didn't really exist; it was all in their minds. Today, we understand how right and wrong they actually were. The pain does exist. I'll just say sensation because quite honestly, it doesn't have to be a pain; it can be an itch or any other feeling. That sensation is as real as anything you and I could ever feel even though the individual may have no arm or leg to transmit the sensation. The pathways have been severed and yet somehow a signal is still reaching the brain – or is it? If there is no arm then there is no extremity to capture information and pass it along to the brain. So where does it come from? The truth of the matter is that such a sensation originates in the brain; a phantom pain is virtually a sensation derived entirely from memory. As long as the mind can imagine it, the body can feel it. Think of how powerful and engrossing the human mind is that it can create a sensation purely from memory and you feel it as you would a hot breath on the back of your neck. That's actually quite amazing. Let's take it one step further.

HOW PAIN WORKS

If our every sensation is nothing more than an electrical impulse flowing through the body that the brain interprets then we must conclude that pain is only pain when the brain translates that electrical impulse as pain. What this means is if the signal never reaches the brain then the brain would never interpret the signal and in all actuality the individual should not feel pain. This means no matter how much pain the body *should feel*, if the brain does not interpret the signal as pain or if the signal never reaches the brain, we would never feel it.

This simple deduction is exactly how some pain medications work. Once the medication is introduced to the body it dampens or blocks the receptors that receive the impulse to the brain and we end up feeling nothing or much less than what we actually should feel. After a time, when the medication begins to wear off, the signal is allowed to reach the brain uninhibited and the pain returns.

There is a condition that is closely related to diabetes called Peripheral Neuropathy. Peripheral Neuropathy is a disease process that affects the peripheral nervous system – the nerves which carry signals to and from the brain and spinal cord to the outermost parts of the body. This condition can lead to pain, weakness, numbness and even a complete loss of sensation most commonly in the hands and feet. A person with peripheral neuropathy could quite literally hold their hand in an open flame and carry on a conversation as though nothing were happening; they would smell the scent of their own charred flesh before they would feel the slightest bit of pain.

What we should hopefully glean from all this is that the human brain is an amazingly wonderful and complex creation, packed full of God-given capabilities that most of us have not even dreamed of delving into and what we just discussed isn't even the tip of the iceberg when it comes to all the things the brain is capable of. I present this information so that we can understand something of grave importance – the Truth. The Truth is that the mind is *the person*. No matter what our bodies look like or how they function, you and I are not our bodies. Our bodies, according to Genesis 2:7 are nothing more than the dust of the earth that we are encased in. Our bodies are simply a vehicle to drive information to the brain for it to interpret as we navigate our way through life. Our bodies are, therefore, an extension of our brains. The human body is a tool that the brain uses to gather information. Let's push this envelope just a little bit further.

GOD'S INVESTMENT

Let's take a look at an excerpt from a chapter of my book, *Redefining Love*. We pick up right after the reading of the Parable of the Talents, found in Matthew 25:14-30, you can read that passage over to reacquaint yourself with the parable if you like but it's not the parable that I'm interested in at the moment. This excerpt helps to relay a simple understanding that I actually think is quite profound. It just so happens to align perfectly with what we just discussed about the brain. Take a look:

This scripture vividly expresses a simple truth: where an investment is made, a positive return is expected. We all know this. People make investments virtually every minute of the day and everyone expects their investment to yield a positive return – this is an expectation, not a guarantee. Every investment involves risk and everyone involved in investing understands that a positive return is never a guarantee. Even for God, a positive return on His investment is not guaranteed. The return that God seeks, though, does not rely on the Stock Market but upon you and me.

Of course, there are many lessons within the confines of this parable but we cannot overlook that main point. God has a stake in us and we have a responsibility to make good on His investment. To get a good understanding of God's investment in man, we have to go back to the beginning where it was first recorded. It says in Genesis 2:7:

> *The Lord God formed the man from the dust of the ground and breathed into his nostrils the breath of life, and the man became a living being.*

This is an important scripture because it makes two crucial points that every human being should know:

1. *Man was formed from the dust of the ground.*
2. *The 'breath of life' caused us to become living beings.*

God formed man from the dust of the ground. Our bodies are dust and to the dust, they will return. Our bodies are not our own, they belong to the earth and will return to the earth. In a sense, our bodies are on loan, they are borrowed goods. Your body was taken from the earth and it will return to the earth. Your body is only in your possession for a little while.

Number two alerts us to the fact that the only thing that separates us from a pile of dirt is the breath of life God placed within us – it came from Him. We became living beings only after God breathed life into us. Therefore, the soul, the very life force within, is the breath of God. We live by His inspiration. He deposited His breath into us and gave us life. That breath of life is God's deposit, the investment that He has placed within us. The return on that investment is a life of Love. It is so simple; yet in its simplicity, the answer eludes us. As in the Parable of the Talents, the breath of life that God deposited in us is an individual investment – the investment is life – and He will return to settle accounts with each one of us individually. This means that your life, your soul, is not yours, it is God's, and one day you will be required to give account for the life He has given you. God expects a positive return on His investment and a positive return on the life he has loaned us is Love.

Think about it, if your body belongs to the earth and your soul – your life – is God's then what is actually yours?

The only thing that could possibly be yours is . . . well, choice. You must choose what you will do with the life you have received. In essence, we are all a decision waiting to be made. We are nothing more than a choice between Love and hatred; everything in life is designed to get you to make that decision. Solomon knew this that is why he said in Ecclesiastes 12:6-8:

Remember him – before the silver chord is severed, or the golden bowl is broken; before the pitcher is shattered at the spring, or the wheel broken at the well, and the dust returns to the ground it came from, and the spirit returns to God who gave it. "Meaningless! Meaningless!" says the Teacher. "Everything is meaningless!"

Everything truly is meaningless! Once we understand that our bodies and our senses are simply an extension of our brains and our brains are nothing more than a tool to gather and decipher information in order to make the decision that we all face, it becomes clear that the only thing that truly matters is the decision – the Choice we all must make on whether we are going to love God or hate Him. Everything else is meaningless. Satan completely understands this concept and that is why he fights so hard to make us and keep us slaves in our own minds, clouded and confused; distracted from the truth. He craftily attempts to occlude the Path of Righteousness until all that remains are the many *Roads of Rebellion.* He clouds the decision hoping that we would never be able to see through the fog and realize life is by far simpler than we believe it is. He then completely confuses our concept of love so that even if we *choose* to love God, we won't love Him *as He defines love* as is stated in John 13:34-35 but according to our own jaded understanding of love which is actually more akin to hatred. Satan leaves nothing to chance. He actively seeks out our destruction at every turn. We must actively seek out righteousness at every turn or it is our fate to fall victim to one of his many schemes.

SEVEN:

"You will never be free until you free yourself from the prison of your own false thoughts."

– Philip Arnold

THE BATTLEFIELD

TWO FIGHTERS ENTER THE ring pumped and ready for battle. The crowd is screaming; camera lights flash in the darkness like distant stars twinkling in the night sky. Each fighter's team is in their respective corner pumping up the crowd and encouraging their fighter. The fighters themselves shake off the pre-fight jitters and work out any last minute kinks in their joints. They're psyched! They can't stand still; they're rearing to go, hungry for that initial bell, famished for the fight! They throw light jabs, rotate their shoulders and twist their necks to and fro in an effort to stay loose. Once the introductions are done, they meet in the middle of the ring for the rules. Between the two of them, they've heard the rules a thousand times before. They don't come to the center of the ring to hear the rules of the match as much as they come to the center of the ring to stare one another down, eye to eye, nose to nose. Each fighter may hear the rules but they are focused on two things: Peering into the eyes of their opponent, looking for any trace of weakness – the slightest kink in their opponent's armor while holding the other's gaze so as to not give off their own hints of fear. Their eyes are steel, unflinching; there isn't the slightest speck of hesitation or reservation and yet the entire fight can be fought, won or lost in this moment. The physical war would soon begin but the most crucial battle takes place before the first bell sounds. Skin may bruise and blood flow under the weight of blows that would break the bones of lesser men but the most crucial battle is fought in the mind. There is more honesty in that moment in the center of the ring than that which is taught in any number of schools across the country; more said in that moment than is said by the Commentators or sports writers throughout the entire battle, though not a single word passes between the two.

The boxing ring is the battlefield for boxers. For humanity as a whole, *the battlefield is the mind.* Your opponent at this juncture is *you.* Your own *Evil Desires* stands across the ring and Satan is in his corner coaching him every step of the way. Whether you are ready or not doesn't matter because Satan doesn't let his fighter wait for the bell. This is how he attacks; this is where he wages his war against humanity and he doesn't often lose. Satan rarely has to lace up his gloves yet his record to date is better than 7 billion to 1. Mano o Mano, *you don't stand a chance.*

What is mindset? Without pulling out a dictionary, one might be able to deduce the meaning by simply looking at the word. Mindset is the way in which one's mind has been set; a cemented train of thought or an unchangeable process of taking in and interpreting information. Such a deduction would not necessarily be spot on but it is close enough to get a general sense of the word. For the sake of my mom, who always forced me to look up a definition rather than deduce my own *(thankfully)*, here is a dictionary definition: *Mindset is a habitual characteristic or mental attitude that determines how you will interpret and respond to situations.*

Here is another definition: *Mindset is a set of assumptions, methods or notations that is so established that it creates a powerful incentive to continue to adopt or accept prior behaviors, choices or tools. This phenomenon is also sometimes described as mental inertia, groupthink or a paradigm, and it is often difficult to counteract its effects upon analysis and the decision making process.*

Mindset can be viewed as the Owner's Manual of the mind. In a sense, one can say that mindset is the methodology by which one interprets and processes information and ultimately draws conclusions. It is the internal perspective and perception that leads each individual down the path of choices they make. Mindset is the sum of our core beliefs, realizations and understanding; it is the answer to every question of motivation; the *"how"* and *"why"* of every human achievement. Mindset is the reason that some give up at the same point when others dig in their heels and stand firm. Individual resolve or desire may come to mind and I would not argue with either of those answers but what we must understand is that it is Mindset that creates both desire and resolve. Your mindset is who you are at the core of your being. Your mindset is *you.*

Every action is formulated by mindset because it is the mindset that determines what is and is not possible; what you will and will not do – your breaking point and your point of no return. Mindset can liberate one person and enslave another with the same belief; it can make one person stare fearlessly into the eyes of opposition and make another melt with fear into the spaces in the floorboards. Your mindset is you. Your mindset is the sum of your convictions.

MINDSET BEGINS

Mindset is shaped largely by our convictions but there are many things that affect our convictions, including but not limited to environment, experiences, lessons learned and that which has been taught and understood to be or accepted as truth as well as the sum of our fears, doubts and even the things to which we are ignorant. Many factors play a part and each one can alter you just enough to make your particular mindset uniquely your own. We all have had very different experiences, perspectives and influences so it is safe to say that no two people have the exact outlook or mindset because no two people have the exact experience; even twins are individuals and may come to completely different conclusions from similar situations. We may have similar dispositions but each person's ultimate mindset will vary even if just slightly from one to another. In the end, we find that belief and experience weighs greatly upon mindset, even more so than other factors like environment and such. I mean, let's be honest, the average rational adult does not spend countless hours contemplating that which he or she does not believe is at least remotely possible and even if the individual has a strong belief in whatever it is they are contemplating, without some form of positive reinforcement, the dream will eventually die.

Before the first plane took flight, countless contraptions were created to aid man in this endeavor – all failed, yet hope lingered on. The Wright brothers were not guaranteed success but they were armed with a deep-seeded desire to achieve flight based on their faith in the idea that it was possible and the minor successes that they and others had along the way. Even when it seemed fruitless to continue onward, and it certainly must have come to that a time or two, every little glimmer of hope encouraged them to stay the course and the rest is, as they say, history.

Like the two prize fighters squaring off in the center of the ring prior to a fight, we are all engaged in a battle that is first waged and won or lost in our minds. Once you begin to understand mindset and the role it plays in your life, you will begin to see that the single most important enemy you will face is your very own thoughts and attitudes.

EIGHT:

"You are confined only by the walls you have built."

– Andrew Murphy

WHAT THE MIND BELIEVES

I CAME ACROSS A scripture in the King James Version of the Bible that I had not found in any other version. This is not to say that the King James Version is flawed or the other versions are totally inaccurate. This is simply to say that the King James and New King James Versions of the Bible say this line slightly different than the other versions although, ultimately, they all seem to say the same thing. I just so happen to like the way it is worded in the King James Version best. The scripture is:

Proverbs 23:7 (KJV)

> [7]*For as a man thinketh in his heart, so is he . . .*

For my wife, Yasmin, this is a scripture that is near and dear to her heart because her Great Grandfather would quote it all the time when she was a little girl growing up in Jamaica. This scripture has quickly become a source of pleasant memories for my wife and for that reason I have kind of taken to it as well. That's not the only reason, though. As I studied out mindset I began to realize how important this scripture is.

In this simple, little known scripture God gets right to the root of it all by weaving together the deepest thoughts of our hearts and our actions into one inseparable unit. Who you are at the core of your being and what you do are in perfect alignment; they agree completely. This means that your actions reveal who you are; what is truly inside of you; the deep down *"real you"*. Your actions reveal the things you hold most dear; that which you are convinced of at the very core of your being.

We need look no further than a Man's actions to see what he holds most dear in his life. What you value; what you truly believe or what for you has become conviction is a well spring that spews forth from your core in the form of actions. So what you do is directly related to who you are at your core. As a matter of fact, I am convinced that it is utterly impossible to do anything other than that which springs forth from the deepest well of your pure and true convictions. Sure, we can all *keep up appearances* for a time but no matter how hard you try, sooner or later, what is inside – *the real you* – will come bubbling up to the surface like a geyser. No matter how much you try to turn away from who you are, you will always return. You can't escape who you are; you can only mask it for a time. No matter how much effort you put into changing your behavior, you will remain who you are at your core because you are trying to change from the outside in rather than from the inside out. Because your actions reveal your convictions, the true enemy is not your actions as much as it is your heart – your convictions. To truly change your actions, you must change who you are at your core; you must change *your convictions.* Trying to change your actions without changing your convictions is like treating the symptoms rather than the ailment itself. You don't treat a heart attack with Tylenol. The pain may diminish somewhat but you are ultimately still on the verge of death. You attack the ailment and the symptoms will go away. To change your actions without a change of heart will ultimately lead to a continuous, lifelong struggle to be something you know deep down in your heart you are not which only results in inner turmoil, anger, frustration and eventually depression. This is one of the main reasons that so many Christians have lifelong struggles with certain sins.

Have you ever thought about how you can give up one sin and never struggle with it again but there are other sins that just seem to ride you and ride you no matter what you do and for how long? We often chalk that one up to the *"Condition of Man"* without first considering that we were able to give up other sins that had an equal hold on us before. So is it really the *"Condition of Man"* why we tend to continue in one sin over another or is that simply a convenient excuse?

God says: *As a man thinks in his heart, so is he.* We can't resolve to simply sweep the thoughts and sins of our hearts under a rug – we will never change that way. They must be eliminated; eradicated from our hearts entirely; purged from within through the introduction of new convictions which breeds new actions or they will rise back to the surface and show you who you really are. Sins that just continue to keep rearing their ugly heads no matter how much advice, prayer, *"laying on of hands"* or anointings you receive are in your life because you want them there. We have to understand and accept that fact before we can move on. There can be no progress in moving within the Jesus Mindset without acknowledging and taking responsibility for the sin in your life.

You can break a bottle of incense and myrrh over someone's head if you want to; *without a change in that person's convictions, their actions will remain the same because your actions are a direct result of the convictions you hold dear at the core of your being.* Therefore, each one of us is limited by the convictions we have and hold near and dear at the core of our being. Simply put, *you are, at this very moment, the result of what you have become convinced of over the course of your life*; whether that's good, bad or somewhere in the middle, that is who you have become but that is not who you were created to be.

FOR ARGUMENT'S SAKE

Now before we go any further, just so that we can be clear that we are not making assumptions about the meaning of Proverbs 23:7 or attempting to take it out of context, let's take a look at the scriptures around it. I will also do a comparison between the New King James and the New International Versions of the Bible to show that the meaning doesn't change from one version to another although the wording is different. Below we have the same passage of scripture taken from the NIV and the NKJV of the Bible.

Proverbs 23:6-8 (NKJV)

[6]Do not eat the bread of a miser, nor desire his delicacies; [7]for as he thinks in his heart, so is he. "Eat and drink!" he says to you, but his heart is not with you. [8]The morsel you have eaten, you will vomit up, and waste your pleasant words.

Proverbs 23:6-8 (NIV)

[6]Do not eat the food of a begrudging host, do not crave his delicacies; [7]for he is the kind of person who is always thinking about the cost. "Eat and drink," he says to you, but his heart is not with you. [8]You will vomit up the little you have eaten and will have wasted your compliments.

As far as a comparison of versions goes, both texts are issuing the same warning: *do not be deceived by the words of a miser or his generosities, the thoughts that occupy his mind reveal who he truly is and though he beckons you to partake of his bounty, he is begrudgingly watching everything you eat, thinking only of the cost. The little you have eaten, you will regret for he will demand as much in return.*

Looking at verses six through eight, we can see that these surrounding verses do not change the meaning of verse seven. *For as he thinks in his heart, so is he,* simply means that the way an individual presents themselves may not necessarily be who they are on the inside. What you can infer from this is *who you are deep down, on the inside, is who you really are regardless of what may be presented on the surface.* Do you see that? This means that *our truth* is found in what lies beneath. *Who we are at our core is who we truly are.* Now if we approach this from a *Perspective of Power we see that we are who we are at our core but we do not have to stay that person; we can change. If we change who we are at our core, we truly change who we are and who we can become!* Thus we confirm the conclusion that *we are limited only by our convictions and our actions are a direct result of those convictions.*

AMUSING REFLECTIONS

I saw an image online of a small fishbowl with a goldfish swimming around in it with a huge shark dorsal fin strapped to its back. The caption read: *You are what you think!* I smiled when I saw the meme and then wondered to myself, what if we really believed that. What if you looked at that image and thought to yourself: *"That's true. I can be the shark!"* Is a goldfish suddenly going to turn into a shark because it believes it's a shark? I doubt it. Can you radically change because you believe in the power of God working through you? Can you completely transform into a different version of yourself who no longer falls into the same traps and pitfalls as before because you are aware of and acknowledge the presence of God within you and the awesome might He has left at your disposal? I say, *"Why not?"*

I came across another image; this one was of a kitten gazing into a puddle at its reflection. The reflection gazing back at the cute little kitten was that of a ferocious, full grown, male lion. I had the same reaction viewing this picture as I did the first one – I smiled every time I saw it until God showed me my sin.

There was a problem with my response to the picture that eluded me for months. I had the picture on my phone and every so often I would be drawn to it and just stare at it for a while. God was asking me: *Why do you find this funny? Why does this picture amuse you?* I would think, because it is a cute picture or because it is silly. The question kept coming back to me. It had me going for a little while before I finally realized that the picture was not silly. I found it amusing to see this little kitten gazing into the water and seeing a lion looking back because deep down it was impossible. I didn't see anything but my reflection when I looked in the mirror. I saw no lion inside. I found it improbable to see that much depth. When I looked into a mirror, seeing a lion was the furthest thing from my mind but God was telling me there was more to me than I realized. He was telling me to look deeper; to dig deeper and He would give me a glimpse of reality. God was telling me that there was far more to me than I've been willing to see because I, like the world, was choosing to see myself through my actions. We have to learn to dig deeper: *deeper into ourselves, deeper into the Word and deeper into our relationship with God.* You and I are not the sum of our actions – that is what Satan wants us to believe. This is the way the world views each other but this is not the way that God views us or wants us to view others. I may have, because of the sum of my decisions, become less but that is not who I am. God was using those pictures to show me that there was a lion inside of me; He knows because He put it there. The same is true for you. You are more than you have come to believe.

WE ARE MORE

There is a great line in the movie The Lion King when the spirit of Musafa tells his son, in the powerful, thundering voice of James Earl Jones, *"You are more than you have become!"* I believe God is saying the very same thing to us, today: *we are more than we have become*. We need to dig deeper, knowing that God is waiting to pour into us *more*; He is waiting to reveal *more*. He was trying to show me something that I would have never come to understand on my own. He was showing me the value I placed in His heart. He was showing me the trust and hope He had for me why He was willing to place His Holy Spirit within me. He was showing me that in His eyes I was worth the sacrifice. He was showing me that *when God looks at us, He doesn't see the kitten; He sees the lion! He sees the lion because it is He who put it in us. He sees the lion because that is what He created. He sees the lion that most of us will never become because rather than the lion, all we can see is the guck, slime and grime we've made of our lives; the guck, slime and grime that God has already forgiven.*

We are not the sum of our mistakes; we are more than that. We don't see ourselves for who we are; we see ourselves for what we've become but we are more than even that and we need to know this; we need to realize this and accept it. We are more because He has forgiven us. We are more because He has restored us. We are more because He has adopted us as His Sons and Daughters. We are more because He has called us His Children. We are more! So be more! It's time to shake off the excuses. Jesus never gave excuses and neither did He accept them. The Mindset of Christ is *excuse-free*. It's a *"put up or shut up"* mentality. You take responsibility for your life, your thoughts, and your actions; you take responsibility for *you* because you were made to be *more*. He calls us His Children; it's time we started living up to that.

We are not kittens looking in the water failing to see lions; we are lions looking into the water seeing only kittens! Do you see how great Satan's deception is? Do you see how great the Lord's love and patience is? We are not mere men – *if there even is such a thing* – we are more! We are the *Sons and Daughters of the Living God!* We need to stop denying who we are and stop making excuses for what we have and continue to make of ourselves. This was Jesus' conviction about Himself but more importantly, this is His conviction about *you and me*. In Matthew 12:46-50, He calls us His sisters and brothers, mothers and fathers. We are Jesus' siblings; fellow heirs – princes and princesses of the Kingdom of God. We are not strangers or even invited guests; *we are jumping-on-the-couch-and-running-through-the-halls-children!* God claims us as His; we need to equally claim Him as our own and as it says in Ephesians 4:1, *live a life worthy of the calling you have received.* When this becomes our conviction it will become manifest in our lives but first we need to plain and simple *believe it*.

NINE:

"If you always put limits on everything you do, physical or anything else, it will spread into your work and into your life. There are no limits. There are only plateaus and you must not stay there, you must go beyond them."

– Bruce Lee

COMMON UNDERSTANDING FAILS

WE ARE THE SONS and Daughters of the Living God but we do not believe this so we do not acknowledge and honor our lineage, our heritage, in our daily lives. Jesus *knew who He was*. Jesus knew He was God's Son and acknowledged that every day. He was well aware of His lineage; He was well aware of who His Father was and whom He represented. He knew that God loved Him and He knew what it meant to Love God and He not only loved God but others as God Loved Him.

There is no mistake about it; Jesus knew many things that many of us Christians do not even believe and that alone creates a huge chasm between our mindset and His.

We all have opinions about things. We all have beliefs. We all have things that we know; things we are certain or convinced of beyond the shadow of doubt. What we probably do not realize is what we choose to place in each of those compartments not only affects our lives but it ultimately affects our relationship with God as well. In order to know what goes where, we must first label the compartments and understand the differences between each one. The compartments are: *Opinions, Beliefs and Conviction.*

What does it mean to *believe*? What does it mean to have an *opinion*? What does it mean to be *convinced*? According to the Merriam-Webster Dictionary the definition of *Believe* is: *to accept something as true; to have a firm conviction as to the goodness, efficacy, or ability of something or to have an opinion.*

What do you think about that definition? Does that clear it up for you? Did you notice what it said, there? It says *to believe* is to have a *firm conviction* and in the same breath it also says it is *to have an opinion!* To use both words to define belief is to say all three words mean the same thing. Since when did conviction and an opinion mean the same thing?

In that same dictionary, an *Opinion* is defined as: *a view, judgment or appraisal formed in the mind about something; a generally held view.* Conviction or *to convince*, in that same dictionary is defined as: *to cause someone to believe that something is true; to overpower with persuasion.*

So if you are the one *convinced* or the one *with conviction*, what this means is that you are the individual *overpowered by persuasion*. You are the one persuaded by an overpowering amount of evidence. An opinion needs no evidence, at all. An opinion is not formed by the amount of evidence provided; it is simply a view. Even in the same dictionary the definitions of these two words are totally different yet both of them are used to define the word *believe*. That doesn't make much sense.

Here is another definition I found for the word *Believe* and this one seems to ring true. It says, to believe is: *confidence in the truth or existence of something not immediately susceptible to rigorous proof.* The key words in this definition are: *not immediately susceptible to rigorous proof.* This means that a belief doesn't have to be proven. As long as you believe it is true, that is all that is needed for the belief to exist; right or wrong. An example of this would be*: I believe in God.* I don't need proof of any kind to believe in God. I simply need to accept His existence as truth and I am a believer. Though my beliefs are undefined, I am, for all intent and purposes, *a believer*. I don't have to change one thing about myself or expect anything different than what I've expected of myself all along. In other words, I don't have to change one bit – as long as I believe I am a believer. Belief does not equate to change nor does it elicit change. This is a word that we, unfortunately, confuse greatly. Too often we believe and teach that *a believer* is something more than a person who simply possesses a belief. We have to grasp this. Being a *believer* simply means that you believe, nothing more. *What you believe or the affects your belief has on your life, if it affects it at all, are unimportant because none of those things need to be present in order for belief to exist.*

I can say that *I believe I can fly* but that does not mean that I can. Stating my belief in something does not make the belief true. That statement does not change me in any way, shape or form. I am simply stating a belief and doing so truly means nothing in the grand scheme of things. My belief in my ability to fly does not even mean that I will make an attempt to fly at any point in time in my life. All it means is . . . *I believe I can fly.*

As long as my beliefs are unchallenged, I can carry them to the grave intact – whether they are right or wrong. A belief needs no special proof or evidence of any kind, at all, in order to exist; it simply needs to be stated and accepted as truth *by the believer.*

An opinion needs no special proof either. Where the two differ is in the fact that an opinion doesn't need to be accepted as truth by anyone whereas the belief needs to be accepted as truth by the believer. An opinion is simply a view, position or a thought that could possibly be true or have some truth in it. Where opinions are concerned, the jury's out. An opinion is not completely believed even by the person who has the opinion and is therefore open to and subject to change if a new opinion emerges that seems more plausible.

FROM BELIEF TO CONVICTION

What we have here are not two words that define *belief* but three words that details an individual's progression from one to the other; from opinion to belief and from belief to conviction. Most everyone has an opinion about God, even if that opinion is that He does not exist. Regardless of the opinion you may have, it must be noted that an *opinion* does not require acceptance as truth and needs absolutely no evidence to exist; it simply needs to be stated and/or generally held by an individual. *Belief*, on the other hand, requires that the believer accept it as truth – although there need not be any evidence of its existence. *As long as the believer believes, belief exists.* Now *conviction* is a beast of a different kind. Conviction is confirmed in the eyes of the believer *through the preponderance of evidence.* So conviction is created through a process. Anyone can have an opinion. To believe requires some trust in whatever it is you believe. Conviction requires proof! *Conviction only exists when the belief has been verified through life experience.*

Now in order to get from belief to conviction, we need to add another compartment in there. How can something be proven if it is never tested? In order for conviction to exist, the belief must be challenged and put to the test. Anyone can have a belief but in order for conviction to develop, you have to put your money where your mouth is. You have to prove you believe what you claim to believe. The compartment we're talking about that would be jarred between belief and conviction; is *faith.* You cannot move from belief to conviction without faith because faith is defined as *belief in action.* The moment you put belief to the test, it ceases to be belief – *it becomes faith.*

If I were to say that I think Man can fly, that would be an opinion. I don't have to believe it; it's just a statement. If I say that I believe I can fly, that's a little different. This is a belief but it is only a belief – nothing more, until the belief is tested. Once I jump into the air in hopes of soaring through the skies, I am putting my belief to the test.

Jumping in the air would be an act of faith. Once faithful action is initiated God has an opportunity to either confirm or deny that faith through life experience. The moment I take flight and soar through the clouds, my act of faith has been confirmed and faith has given way to conviction. Once I have proven that I can fly, no one can ever tell me that I can't. Therefore, acting upon a belief is faith; and the confirmation of your faith is conviction.

THE CATALYST OF FAITH

Mindset begins to take shape the moment we come out of the womb and begin to understand and contemplate the world around us. Our mindset is formed as we learn from our parents and our environment; the associations we make as well as the things we hold on to and accept as truth. Out of this jumble of experiences, lessons, successes and failures, comes desire. Once desire sees the light of day, our Perceived Reality will either crush it underfoot or foster its growth. Desire is *the Catalyst of Faith.* Without desire there is no drive to see your beliefs come to fruition. Without desire beliefs fade. And desire is only birthed after mindset has deemed it possible.

Does a child come out of the womb wanting to become a doctor, lawyer, fireman or policeman? I would think not. An infant has no concept of occupations until the parent or someone else introduces the idea to them. Once the idea is introduced and the mindset deems it possible, the real possibility of the idea fosters the birth and growth of desire and desire influences action or faith. If mindset determines the desire unreasonable, it will either take a place on the backburner until circumstances change or die altogether.

My sister is a medical doctor and I can remember when she was barely two or three years old, when asked what she wanted to be when she grew up, she would always say – *before she could even pronounce the word properly* – a pediatrician. She didn't come out of the womb saying that. She was not born with this desire. Somewhere along the way, it was introduced to her and she latched on to it. Maybe it was mom or dad that first said it to her; maybe it was her pediatrician. I'm not sure but the idea was introduced to her and she accepted it as a viable possibility. The desire was encouraged by the whole family and this reinforced the possibility, cementing it in – this was no pipe dream; the more encouragement she received as she grew the more this reality materialized. Had she not believed that achieving her doctorate in Medicine was possible, she would have never pursued it. So mindset not only determines desire but assesses value, determining just how far you are willing to go to see that desire through to fruition. I remember the sleepless nights that seemed to come a week at a time. The toll it took on her body was incredible – I didn't know you could get black and blue bags under your eyes from a prolonged lack of sleep! I remember the talks Yasmin and I had with her as the weight bore down upon her as she felt she wasn't strong enough or smart enough to make it. I remember the freak accidents and discouragements that could have and probably should have sidelined her. One time she was sitting in her car studying before church and *"something"* told her to take a break from studying and go inside a little early and fellowship. She stepped out of the car and before she made it to the church door, a huge tree fell over and flattened the car. Crazy incidents like this had become such a normal part of our lives that when she looked back at the car she was just sitting in flattened beneath a tree, she simply sighed and continued inside the church building to fellowship.

Today, she is a doctor but I wouldn't say that she became a doctor because of sheer will and desire. I would say, and I believe she would agree, that she became a doctor because every situation, every experience she went through was molding and shaping her into the doctor she would become. I believe that desire is the catalyst of faith but I believe it is God who pricks our desires initially but as mindset is molded and convictions are formed new desires can encroach upon design just as Perceived Reality encroaches upon Actual Reality attempting to crush it and oust it altogether. I truly believe that this was God's intention for her life. We all go through ups and downs; we're not going to escape that and I don't believe it should be our desire to try to avoid the difficult times. The question is what are these experiences attempting to create within us? I believe that hardships were never designed to break us; they were designed to steel our resolve just like the child stumbling while learning to walk. The problem is that we often break long before we have reached our limit because we have learned to give up; we have learned that it is okay to fold when things get particularly tough rather than stand your ground and forge a way through.

If your mindset is such that views hardships as bumps along the path, you will choose to not lose sight of the goal and endure. If you view hardships as a sort of punishment or wall – the Hand of God telling you, *"This far and no further"* – then you will grumble and complain and ultimately lose sight of the goal or allow the hard times to diminish the desire you once had; ultimately, you will allow circumstances to *devalue your goal.* If something is worth it you will bleed for it; if something is not, you won't lift a finger to fight for it. In the end, we often find that most times we wind up resisting what God is trying to create within us and we are working against God in receiving the desires of our hearts; desires He would love to fulfill but because of our Mindsets; because we have no resolve and fight for so little because we don't value the training it takes to prepare us to become the Children He desires, those dreams will never come to fruition.

THE PATH OF TRANSFORMATION

We change when our actions change and our actions only change when our convictions change. The process through which we change our convictions is called *The Path of Transformation.*

Every relationship is either progressive or regressive and a relationship with God is no different. You are either progressing towards a deeper relationship with God or regressing towards the dissolution of that relationship. If your relationship with God is not progressing towards a deeper relationship then you need to wonder if it is God you have a relationship with or your own opinion of Him. God expects your knowledge of Him as well as your relationship with Him to grow deeper every day. We should all be progressing beyond the point of *opinion* in the direction of *deep convictions.*

Our opinions can be as fleeting as a random thought and often they are. Anything that we read, watch, witness, hear or experience can influence our thoughts and opinions. Most of these opinions die as just that – opinions. The danger is not the influence that life has over your opinions as much as it is the opinions you allow to become beliefs. As opinions are explored, we should begin to recognize the truth or folly therein. The foolishness is cast aside but the bits and pieces we consider truth we hold onto and over time they can become our beliefs.

As was previously stated, a belief needs nothing to exist other than the believer stating that they believe. A belief can stay right there for the duration of an individual's life and demand nothing more of them. It *can* do that; but a belief can also grow; a belief can grow and require the believer to dig deeper into themselves and what it is they claim to believe. You see, the more we *believe* our beliefs, the more real they become to us; the more pressing they become in our lives; the more space they occupy in our minds, so to speak. The more vested we become in our beliefs, the more they begin to play out in our lives; at that point, *faith becomes inevitable because the moment our beliefs manifest into action, belief becomes faith.*

Faith is the proving ground for beliefs. Faith is the kiln through which the impurities of your beliefs are burned away until all that remains are raw convictions. This step is very important to understand because we can often misrepresent what it means to be *faithful.* The act of *acting on your belief is faith.* This means that living faithfully is not just about going to church on the weekends; *living faithfully is living out your beliefs every day.* Being faithful is to practice your belief like the pianist practices the piano until there is no longer any delineation between the individual and his craft; like a marriage, the two become one

– it is the union of faithful living and repetition within the individual that gives birth to conviction and conviction creates mindset.

If we place faith into something and it proves untrustworthy, we usually do not continue to pursue it. As trust wanes so goes belief. If our faith is confirmed through action, trust grows and faith transforms. Through faith, the result of our efforts becomes evidence for us that our belief is true. As this occurs, our faith lays the groundwork for a new reality as it gives way to conviction.

Once conviction is formed it is like a small seedling that needs to grow roots deep into our hearts and minds before it can bring forth new life in the form of actions – an unshakeable tree. As conviction becomes cemented in our psyche, it creates a new *deeper level* of faith and exploration as we continue to *"now more confidently"* live out our beliefs – in a sense, it makes our ceiling our floor, giving us a new level of faith to tread and a deeper level of conviction to aspire to. As conviction is continually confirmed through our lives it begets deeper convictions. It is like we are allowing our brains to *marinate* in these new convictions so it gets into every nook and cranny and really soaks it up. This deeper level of conviction is what *"rewrites our DNA"* creating the new desired actions that occur almost naturally, *without conscious thought.*

Every newly formed deep conviction creates a shift in the mindset; a directional change or transformation. As our mindset transforms, our actions will change to reflect our new convictions. *As our convictions change, we change.* Right or wrong, whether you realize it or not, you are a living, breathing representation of your convictions – what *you consider* truth – just as Jesus was a living, breathing representation of Truth.

The problem most Christians have is that we tend to change our actions without changing our convictions which only yields temporary change. In order to truly change, to transform, we must change our mindset. In order to change our mindset, we must change our convictions. In order to change our convictions we must adopt new beliefs that we will *faithfully adhere to.* But before we can adopt these new beliefs, we must first allow ourselves to come face to face with what we currently believe and hold in our hearts as truth; the motivations behind our beliefs and the built-in limitations that hold us back.

TEN:

"Faith is doubt."

– Emily Dickinson

DEFINED BY DOUBT

THERE IS ONE THING that every step along the Path of Transformation has in common: *they are all measured in accordance with doubt.* All of these terms are defined by the presence of doubt. This means that your opinion about God, your belief in God, faith in God and even the convictions you have about God are all measured or determined by the amount of doubt present. It is virtually a scale that graduates from one to the next, from the lowest to the highest point; from opinion to conviction. The more you doubt the further down the scale you slide. The further down the scale you slide, the less evidence there is in your life of the beliefs you claim to have or the less you are convinced of what you claim to believe. The less you doubt, obviously, the greater the faith, the deeper the convictions; the more evidences in your life of that which you believe. Jesus did not doubt so it would be safe to say that He had more than an opinion about God. Was Jesus a believer? He most certainly believed in God but His understanding went far beyond the limitations of the word belief. Even to say that Jesus had faith feels like a gross misrepresentation because faith is essentially the testing of your belief – seeing whether it is true or false. Does the Bible ever mention Jesus having faith? Think about that. To my knowledge, it doesn't. There isn't a single place in the Bible that speaks of Jesus having or requiring faith. Now, Jesus spoke about the faith of others but He never referred to His own. Why? It doesn't mention Jesus having faith because Jesus did not simply have faith in God; Jesus knew God. He was one with God and that's a whole different level than faith. Even when it comes to convictions anyone can see that Jesus exhibited deep convictions but to say that Jesus was convinced feels inaccurate because in order to be convinced of something, doubt had to be present at some point in time and Jesus most certainly did not doubt God's existence at any point in time. Jesus knew God and God knew Jesus. Jesus knew who He was in the grand scheme of things and accepted one hundred percent the role He would play and the fact that He was God's One and Only.

THE EXISTENCE OF DOUBT

Imagine you are traveling cross country and you come upon a *"mom and pop"* diner that you've never been to before with free standing chairs rather than booths. When you are asked to take a seat, do you assess the chair's sturdiness before sitting or do you simply sit? Do you stop and consider whether the chair can hold your weight or do you sit knowing it will hold you up? Most people would simply sit because they assume that the chair will hold their weight and even if we do assess the chair, we are giving it a quick once over and taking a seat, not a full inspection. Honestly, most people don't even think about it. This assumption is so natural that we sit in every chair without the slightest reservation; without the slightest thought of it crumbling under us regardless of our size. I have been to many Barnes & Noble's Bookstore Cafes, Starbucks and the like and I've seen literally hundreds if not thousands of people take seats without considering the durability of the seat they take. We would actually be shocked if the chair collapsed because we are so certain that the chair will hold our weight. Why is that? Why do we have absolute faith in a chair we've never met before in a diner we're entirely unfamiliar with? This occurs because deep down, though most of us don't readily admit it, we understand that some things do not require faith.

Faith is not a constant. Faith is not an ever-flowing consciousness that we get *"caught up"* in. Faith is only needed when doubt is present. Look at it this way: If you were to attempt to sit on a chair that you are familiar with and it has never let you down before, you would sit with confidence. Your life experiences have confirmed your belief that the chair can and will hold your weight. Now if the chair has crumbled under your weight before you might be a little hesitant about sitting on the chair again. That pause, that apprehension would be the reason faith is required. Faith is akin to trust so *faith is only necessary when you've placed trust in something and it has let you down and is now requiring you to place trust in it again.* If the chair has never let you down, why would there be reason for caution? Why would there be reason for doubt? There wouldn't be; there would be no justifiable reason for doubt. In the same manner, if God has never let you down, what justifiable reason is there for doubt? There shouldn't be; there wouldn't be if we *knew* God. If God's presence was a conviction rather than a belief, there would be no doubt in our hearts. We doubt because we don't completely believe. Faith exists because we doubt.

I'll admit there's a small problem with my analogy. In order for someone to determine whether God has let them down, that person must first place trust in Him. Think about it, the only way the chair can let you down is *after* you have made a conscious decision to place your faith in the chair and take a seat! You can't walk into a café and look at the seat and then consider how tired your legs are and claim the chair has failed you. If you've never placed your butt in the seat and allowed it to hold your full weight then you've never *completely* trusted the chair. *Only after you sit in the chair and it falls apart can you say that the chair has failed you.* If you lack trust for any other reason the fault lies in you. So if someone has never trusted God completely with their life then they've never given God the opportunity to fail them. How can someone fail you if you never placed trust in them? That makes no sense. Unless someone has trusted in God completely there is no possible way He could have ever failed them!

I want you to think about this: *As a Christian, have you placed absolute trust in God? Has He ever let you down? Has He ever failed you?* Basically what we're saying is that doubt is based on *past performance* and faith is only necessary when doubt exists. What this means is that if you can't say that you've placed absolute trust in God then you can't say that He has ever failed you. If you cannot honestly say that God has failed you then there is no justifiable reason for doubt to exist in your life. If there is no reason for doubt then there is no justifiable reason for *faith* to exist either. Do you see that? What this means is that even as Christians, many of us only believe to a point; many of us doubt *without justification – we doubt God for no reason at all.*

Okay, that's not entirely true. There is a reason. There is a pretty solid reason why we doubt God as a people and therefore require faith. It's just not a reason that many of us are going to gravitate towards regardless of how much truth there are in the words that follow: *the only reason we would doubt God without cause is because we, like Adam and Eve, have chosen to heed the voice and words of Satan rather than that of God and many of us hold onto those words even as Christians!*

IN THE PRESENCE OF DOUBT

Opinion, belief and faith all exist within the presence of doubt and according to its declining degrees. Conviction is the only one that somewhat lies outside of this spectrum because conviction only exists when doubt has been eliminated. Conviction is *the removal of doubt.*

Now, this does not mean that whatever you are convinced of is right; this simply means that once you are convinced of something – *the preponderance of evidence you have attained suggests something* – and you have, where this topic is concerned, removed doubt or become convinced. When you are convinced, you are firm in your understanding and cannot be swayed. The moment doubt enters, faith is required and conviction is no more.

Hebrews 11:1-2 (NIV 1984)

[1]Now faith is being sure of what we hope for and certain of what we do not see. [2]This is what the ancients were commended for.

Even when we use the definition of faith as defined in the book of Hebrews, we see the same thing. The scriptures say that faith is *being sure of what we hope for . . .* What we *"hope for"* is what is not guaranteed, so faith is being confident in the face of that which is not guaranteed – *doubt.* Even the scriptures support the fact that faith only exists when doubt is present. When we *hope,* there is a chance the situation may not work out in our favor. As long as there remains a chance of a situation working out one way or another, the potential for doubt exists and coupled with that is the potential for faith. Throughout the scriptures we see many individuals who hoped for particular outcomes; sometimes things worked out the way they expected and sometimes it did not. The opportunity is obviously there for both doubt and faith. Those who were considered faithful were commended because in spite of the presence of doubt, they chose to act according to their belief – which is the definition of faith. Let's take a look at two examples.

Deuteronomy 34:1-5 (NIV)

[1]Then Moses climbed Mount Nebo from the plains of Moab to
the top of Pisgah, across from Jericho. There the Lord showed him the
whole land – from Gilead to Dan, [2]all of Naphtali, the territory of
Ephraim and Manasseh, all the land of Judah as far as the
Mediterranean Sea, [3]the Negev and the whole region from the Valley of
Jericho, the City of Palms, as far as Zoar. [4]Then the Lord said to him,
"This is the land I promised on oath to Abraham, Isaac and Jacob when
I said, 'I will give it to your descendants.' I have let you see it with your
eyes, but you will not cross over into it."

[5]And Moses the servant of the Lord died there in Moab, as the
Lord had said.

I am certain Moses hoped to enter the Promised Land but that was not meant to be. He led the Israelites out of captivity in Egypt and wandered in the desert for forty years as a generation of unbelievers died; all to lead God's people to the edge of the Promised Land and go no further. He was only able to view the Promised Land from a distance. Though God performed many miraculous wonders through Moses and chose him to lead His people out of slavery, God did not allow Moses to enter the Promised Land. In spite of his faith, hope was not realized. The hope Moses had ended on the mountain of the Lord.

Daniel 3:16-18 (NIV)

[16]*Shadrach, Meshach and Abednego replied to him, "King Nebuchadnezzar, we do not need to defend ourselves before you in this matter.* [17]*If we are thrown into the blazing furnace, the God we serve is able to deliver us from it, and he will deliver us from Your Majesty's hand.* [18]*But even if he does not, we want you to know, Your Majesty, that we will not serve your gods or worship the image of gold you have set up."*

Shadrach, Meshach and Abednego all wanted the same outcome; they wanted to live. Whether that meant God intervening and allowing them to walk away unscathed or God intervening as they were tossed into the blazing furnace didn't matter, what was clear is that they wanted to walk away alive but not at the expense of their God. They hoped to walk away from this unfortunate situation they found themselves in and it is clear that they understood that this was not guaranteed. No promises were made that if they stood up to King Nebuchadnezzar God would allow them to survive the King's threat of being thrown into the furnace. They had no assurances as they stood before the King how things would turn out. They all knew the stakes. Their lives were on the line. They believed God *could* save them. That belief was put to the test as they faced the King and the blazing furnace heated up seven times hotter than normal. *Their faith made them stand firm and remember that God could save them.* As they were bound and prepared to be thrown into the blaze, the likeliness of divine intervention must have dissipated some. They *hoped God would rescue them.* Whether He would or He would not was unclear. What was crystal clear was their conviction that whether God did or did not rescue them, they would honor only God and live or die in His name. Their conviction was that God *could rescue them.* Hope, and thus faith, enters because they were not certain that God *would rescue them.*

There are many other stories in the Bible like these two examples and each one presents a similar scenario and the same unspoken truth: *our opinions, beliefs and faith are all measured in accordance with doubt.* In every story, we find someone facing extreme odds. There is a choice to be made and uncertainty looms. The clear path may not seem so clear to the individual facing it but faith dictates their steps through the often great cloud of doubt.

God can do all things and He loves us dearly. Do you believe that is true? Do you believe that God can do all things? Do you believe that He loves you dearly? Are these truths being reflected in your life? Remember that stating that you believe is only acknowledging your belief. *Living in accordance with that belief is faith.* Are you faithful? Are your beliefs being played out in your everyday life?

Our lives should be a continual testing ground for our beliefs; how else will we walk in faith as Jesus commands? How else will we develop deep convictions that will stand the test of time? Only when our beliefs are evident in the lives we lead can we say we are faithful Christians and only then, when faith is made manifest, are convictions formed that will last a lifetime, carrying us through every storm and ultimately into eternity.

ELEVEN:

"Nothing can stop the man with the right mental attitude from achieving his goal; nothing on earth can help the man with the wrong mental attitude."

– Anonymous

ACADEMIA

IN HER BOOK *MINDSET: the New Psychology of Success*, author and Professor Carol S. Dweck, Ph. D., an authority in the study of mindset, states that there are two basic mindsets: *the Fixed Mindset and the Growth Mindset.* She writes in her book that not everyone is entirely one or the other. *As our mindsets form and take shape we move in and out of both mindsets as they pertain to different areas in our lives.* She has also concluded that neither mindset is necessarily better than the other – they are just two different ways of thinking, assessing situations and confronting this world we live in. She says in her book that mindset permeates *every* aspect of life and much of what we think of as personality is actually grown from mindset. Mindset, she says, is what prevents us from fulfilling our potential and at the same time it is the driving force behind our greatest successes. After twenty years of research, Dr. Dweck has come to the conclusion that *the view you adopt for yourself profoundly affects the way you lead your life.* It can determine whether you become the person you want to be or not and whether you accomplish the things you value or whether they remain dreams on the threshing floor. This has led me to believe that mindset plays an immense role in our walk with God, our relationship with God and our relationship with each other.

THE FIXED MINDSET

Believing that your qualities are carved in stone is the *Fixed Mindset.* What does this mean? This means that an individual believes that they or others are born with a certain level of intelligence or character and at best can function at that level. They don't necessarily have to reach that level in their lifetime but they will most certainly max out at that *predetermined level.* Many people will hear this and quickly assume that this is not the way they think but it is not the definition of the term that defines your pattern of thinking but the symptoms or the pattern, itself. This kind of thinking is what led past societies to develop caste systems where a person is born into a particular station and can never rise above that station in life regardless of what fortune befalls them. This is also indicative of the labeling that goes on in our school systems, today. So before you say you do not have a fixed mindset, take a good look at it. Today, if a child scores a ninety-seven on several tests they are considered an "A" student – a bright child. If someone struggles to get seventy-five on the same exams we label the first child smarter than the last without considering circumstances that can affect their test taking abilities. One student is labeled bright while the other is considered average or even borderline. The children adopt this vein of thinking and begin to consider themselves at peak performance *bright, average* or *borderline.* This thinking can carry through the remainder of their lives affecting the outcome of everything they ever attempt. Often, for those who consider themselves average, there is no pressure to overachieve. If your best is a seventy-five, you should feel excited by a seventy-five on a test and ecstatic if you should be lucky enough to score an eighty! You've done what was expected of you! For the students who receive above average grades, the pressure is on to continue to perform at that level, *to prove you're not average.* The below average students, oddly enough, can tend to have the most pressure to perform because no one wants to be considered *"below average".* These students will constantly try to give it their all or go completely to the other side of the spectrum and decide they don't care; they become brazen in their disdain for school and will often act out in class – become the *class clown* to deflect attention away from their poor grades. Some students with a Fixed Mindset are the kind of children that find school or a particular subject difficult and rather than buckle down and learn it, they consider it beyond them and don't waste any further time or effort on that subject. They tell themselves, *"I'm just not a math person"* or say, *"That's just not for me."* When the truth is they never truly gave it a shot because someone told them who they were, they believed it and then it became manifest in their life.

THE GROWTH MINDSET

> *There's another mindset in which these traits are not simply a hand you're dealt and have to live with, always trying to convince yourself and others that you have a Royal Flush when you're secretly worried it's a pair of tens. In this mindset, the hand you're dealt is just the starting point for development. The Growth Mindset is based on the belief that your basic qualities are things you can cultivate through your efforts. Although people may differ in every which way – in their initial talents and aptitudes, interests, or temperaments – everyone can change and grow through application and experience.*
>
> *Do people with this mindset believe that anyone can be anything, that anyone with proper motivation or education can become Einstein or Beethoven? No, but they believe that a person's true potential is unknown (and unknowable); that it's impossible to foresee what can be accomplished with years of passion, toil and training.*

The above is an excerpt from page 13 of Dr. Dweck's book, *Mindset: The New Psychology of Success.* Here we see that the Growth Mindset is different from the Fixed Mindset in that the individual with the Growth Mindset believes that there are no predetermined limits to one's qualities and intelligence. With the Growth Mindset, it is understood that we grow as we go through life. Every experience whether one may deem it good or bad, are experiences that we learn from and add to the flavor of life. With the Growth Mindset you are not continuously trying to prove who you are; you are not seeking reassurance of your value as one would through the Fixed Mindset, you are simply improving and becoming a better version of you. With the Growth Mindset a child will develop an uninhibited curiosity and a love for learning. This is the child that will see the world unfurl before them even though they are not a genius or maybe not even considered bright in the eyes of some – all that doesn't matter because they understand that through dedication and application of self they can achieve. They are not bound by exam grades and possess the fortitude to look a challenge in the eyes and take it on. They will tend to be relentless in their pursuits because they know they are limited only by their will to succeed.

INSIDE THE TWO MINDSETS

The Fixed and the Growth Mindsets both stem from beliefs. In one your qualities and intelligence are predetermined and will lead you down a certain progression of thoughts and actions. The other believes that their qualities and intelligence are cultivated through experiences and dedicated learning and this train of thought will lead the individual down a very different path of thoughts and actions. The Growth Mindset tends to see things through the eyes of some of our favorite clichés: *Nothing ventured; nothing gained* or *if at first you don't succeed, try, try again* or *Rome was not built in a day*. Because these are clichés, it shouldn't surprise us that many with the Fixed Mindset will resort to using these lines as well. The difference between the two is that those with the Growth Mindset believe it and actually act upon their beliefs while those with the Fixed Mindset just say them because they are . . . well, cliché. There is nothing behind the words but more words. The Growth Mindset is more willing to get knocked down and get back up, brush off and keep on moving while the Fixed Mindset will get knocked down and believe the path has come to an end. The people with the Fixed Mindset see things differently. *For them, it's Nothing ventured, nothing lost or if at first you don't succeed you probably didn't have the ability or if Rome wasn't built in a day maybe it just wasn't meant to be. In other words, risk and effort are two things that might reveal your inadequacies and show that you were not up to the task. In fact, it's startling to see the degree to which people with the Fixed Mindset do not believe in effort.*

So you have one set of people that take to life with the notion that growth comes through their experiences and that success through effort makes the journey worthwhile. They don't believe they have anything to prove and are willing to stumble along the path, learning as they go – as a matter of fact, they expect to stumble. You have another set of people that believe that anything that requires effort is just not worth doing. They shouldn't have to exert effort because in their eyes, effort is a sign of weakness or weak mindedness because effort means that you were not born with the ability to excel without it. In the end, they live under an almost constant pressure to perform in order to prove that they are more than they are out of fear that someone may find out the truth. They live in fear. Now remember having a fixed or growth mindset does not mean that you think like this at all times – most of us are a cross between the two, resorting to one or the other at different times or as we approach different things.

When I was in elementary school and even junior high school I excelled in Science and English without studying and considered myself a *"natural"*. In high school and college I continued to do well in English without studying but science had taken a turn. I had to study to do well in Science and began to lose interest in the sciences because it no longer came *"natural"* for me; it required effort. Though I knew nothing of the fixed or growth mindset at the time, I began to exhibit classic signs of the fixed mindset. Eventually this would change but for a short while I lost interest in my science classes because I thought that perhaps it was just no longer *"my thing"*.

Here are a few real life examples taken directly from Dr. Dweck's book to further illustrate the differences between the two Mindsets:

> *The Martins worshipped their 3 y/o Robert and always bragged about his feats. There had never been a child as bright and creative as theirs. Then Robert did something unforgivable – he didn't get into the number one preschool in New York. After that, the Martins cooled toward him. They didn't talk about him the same way, and they didn't treat him with the same sense of pride and affection. He was no longer their brilliant little Robert. He was someone who had discredited*

> *himself and shamed them. At the tender age of three, he was a failure.*

Think about that situation. This is a true story. This had nothing to do with the child's mindset and everything to do with his parents yet this child will grow up scarred because of it. The child, Robert, will grow up with a predetermined mindset written in stone by his parents, because of what they believed. The parents built their child up to be nothing short of Einstein and then when the child experiences a minor setback – he didn't get into the *"school of choice"* – his fall from grace is epic! Imagine being this three year old who in the eyes of his parents is already a failure; a loser; someone who shamed them! That could be crippling to the psyche and to this child's future. He will forever be undeserving and inadequate in his own eyes despite his successes because that is what his parents engrained in him.

The story of Bernard Loiseau is another sad but true tale which emphasizes the downside of mindset:

> *Bernard Loiseau was one of the top chefs in the world. Only a handful of restaurants in all of France receive the supreme rating of three stars from the Guide Michelin, the most respected restaurant guide in Europe. His was one of them. Around the publication of the 2003 Guide Michelin, however, Mr. Loiseau committed suicide. He had lost two points in another guide, going from a nineteen (out of twenty) to a seventeen in the Gault Millau. And there were rampant rumors that he would lose one of his three stars in the new Guide. Although he did not, the idea of failure possessed him.*

> *Loiseau had been a pioneer. He was one the first to advance the "nouvelle cuisine" trading the traditional butter and cream sauces of French cooking for the brighter flavors of the foods themselves. A man of tremendous energy, he was also an entrepreneur. Besides his three-star restaurant in Burgundy, he had created three eateries in Paris, numerous cookbooks, and a line of frozen foods. A man of such talent and originality could easily have planned for a satisfying future with or without the two points or the third star but in the Fixed Mindset, their lower rating gave him a new definition of himself: Failure. Had-been.*

From the outside looking in we can easily assess that the loss of ground in the industry wasn't that deep. But that's only easy to say *from the outside looking in.* We don't know what it's like to be Loiseau. The average person will never know what it's like to excel at that high-level of success in his industry. We can only guess and try to relate or understand. In a world where status is everything and there's no room for second best the loss of those two stars wasn't just a slip up – *it was defining* – at least it was to Mr. Bernard Loiseau.

Legendary basketball coach, John Wooden once said, *"You aren't a failure until you start to blame."* What this means is that you learn from your mistakes when you own them; you learn nothing when you blame others. Maybe that is why God wants us to confess our sins to one another. As long as you own up to them, they are there for you to learn from and grow through. This is a perfect example of the growth mindset.

You are not limited; you are free to explore just how much you can learn and grow.

For me, my Growth Mindset began to kick in once I realized that I could not go further in my chosen field without Science classes. Reluctantly, I had to admit that I needed to learn this stuff and had to admit that I had to study to do so. Facing a wall in Science, I shifted from a Fixed Mindset to a Growth Mindset, albeit reluctantly. Now this was just for my Science classes. That shift in mindset where English was concerned didn't occur until many years later when I decided to try my hand at writing screenplays in early 2000. I went out and bought several books on writing screenplays and writing in general as well as many screenplays and began to study the art. The funny thing is that this transition wasn't nearly as difficult to make as my shift in mindset where Science was concerned in part because I had already seen the fruits of effort and understood that there was a well of potential in each of us. I'd seen the results of transitioning from one mindset to the other and concluded that it was worth the effort.

Now, this is an academic view of mindset and frankly, an extremely generalized view, at that. There's no way I could cram everything that Dr. Dweck learned over twenty years of study in the field into a single chapter. I can only hope I have not done a great disservice to her book in trying to summarize it here. I would recommend reading the book if the study of Mindset is of interest to you. I found Mindset to be an amazing journey into the *"hows"* and *"whys"* behind the things that we do or do not do and I believe these mindsets carry over into our spiritual makeup and thus our relationship with God and each other.

TWELVE:

"Knowing is not enough, we must apply. Willing is not enough, we must do."

– Bruce Lee

WISDOM AND UNDERSTANDING

WHILE WE ARE ON the subject of academia, now would be an opportune time to discuss *Wisdom, Understanding* and *Intellect*. These words have been greatly misconstrued over the years. Wisdom has to do with our relation to God. Intelligence has to do with our understanding of ourselves and the world around us. Let me explain: God's IQ test is quite simple when you think about it. You don't need a number two pencil to take this exam. There aren't dozens of multiple choice questions, essay or fill-in answers. God's IQ test is nothing more than an intense look at each and every individual life and their response to His presence.

Proverbs 9:10 (NIV)

10 *The fear of the Lord is the beginning of wisdom, and knowledge of the Holy One is understanding.*

To fear God is the beginning of wisdom; to know Him is to have understanding. Now it is important to note that God said the *beginning* of wisdom not the fulfilment of it; those are two very different things and we'll get into that in a moment but what we need to understand right here and now is that wisdom begins with the fear of God. Wisdom is the fear of God and continuing in that relationship and coming to know Him is what it means to have understanding. Do you see the progression, there? God is all about progression through growth. He doesn't just throw us to the wolves. He allows us to grow through each situation, handling just a little more than before until we are strong enough to handle arriving where He wanted us all along. When we fight against this progression, we ultimately delay the blessing of our endurance if not go completely off course altogether.

Wisdom and Understanding are the first two rungs on the ladder of your relationship with God. The beginning of wisdom is acknowledging God's existence as the Creator. That is the first step. Once you decide to continue on that path to come to know your Creator, you are on *the Path of Understanding*. As you grow from viewing Him as your Creator to your Father and God, the Lord of your life, your Understanding continues to grow. Thus, Understanding is equated to the depth of your relationship with God. As you grow in your Understanding of God, you grow in your relationship with Him; the depth of your relationship increases. As the depth of your relationship increases, you begin to fall in love with Him. As your love for God increases, your willingness to lose yourself in that love increases. It's a simple progression that ends with oneness and unity in love. Let's break it down a little more.

THE FULFILMENT OF WISDOM

If the fear of the Lord is the *beginning of Wisdom*, what then is the fulfillment of Wisdom? What does it mean to be *wise* according to God? The answer is *Love*. *We progress through Fear and Wisdom to Knowledge and Understanding and from Knowledge and Understanding we progress to Love and Sonship.* Look at these scriptures . . .

John 13:34-35 (NIV)

34"A new command I give you: Love one another. As I have loved you, so you must love one another. 35By this everyone will know that you are my disciples, if you love one another."

John 14: 23 (NIV)

[23]Jesus replied, "Anyone who loves me will obey my teaching. My Father will love them, and we will come to them and make our home with them."

Romans 8:12-16 (NIV)

*[12]Therefore, brothers and sisters, we have an obligation – but it
is not to the flesh to live according to it. [13]For if you live according to the
flesh, you will die; but if by the Spirit you put to death the misdeeds of
the body, you will live. [14]For those who are led by the Spirit of God are
the children of God. [15]The Spirit you received does not make you slaves,
so that you live in fear again; rather, the Spirit you received brought
about your adoption to sonship. And by him we cry, "Abba, Father."
[16]The Spirit himself testifies with our spirit that we are God's children.*

In these three scriptures you see three points that come together to paint a single picture. In the first scripture loving others as Christ has loved us is evidence of our discipleship; love is the badge that shouts to the world that we are His! But note that this is not love as the world knows it; this is not the love that brings couples together only to end in divorce – this is love as defined by the Master, Creator and Perfector of our faith, God, the Holy One of Israel. This is love as Jesus understood and exemplified it. In the second scripture we see obedience enter the equation as God tells us that to love Him is to obey Him and that He will make His home with us. Here we see that God equates loving Him to obeying Him. Contrary to popular understanding this is a conditional statement. God's love for us is unconditional but our love for Him is measured by obedience and He will make His home with those who love Him. This means that though He loves us all, He will *only* make His home with *those who love Him*; *those who prove they love Him.* If you claim to love Him, He says in 1 John 4:21, that *you must love others.* This is not speaking of merely acknowledging His existence but faithful obedience to His word – to love others as He loves us. The third scripture pulls it all together in Sonship. It shows us that once we are led by the Spirit of God, we are no longer bound by fear – *fear falls away from the equation because fear is only the beginning* – it is necessary but only to a point. Fear is a phase we must go through but it is a phase we must move beyond. Through His grace we become His adopted children and even better than that, the Spirit Himself testifies on our behalf that we are the Children of God! The Spirit cannot lie; so what the Spirit testifies is Truth. We are Sons and Daughters of the Holy One; we are God's Children.

Fear of the Lord may be the beginning of Wisdom but *loving God and being obedient in loving others as He has loved us is Wisdom and Understanding in its entirety*; to acknowledge God, to respond to the love that He has shown us and to return it to Him in our willingness to lose ourselves in the act of loving others as He loves us is the completion or fulfilment of Wisdom and Understanding. This means that absent God, there is no Wisdom or Understanding. Wisdom and Understanding is not found outside of a relationship with God.

INTELLIGENCE

There are wildly intelligent people in this world and no one is questioning the intelligence of human beings but without acknowledging God – *without love* – all of our intelligence stands only to condemn us and leads to our coming undone as a people.

Genesis 11:5-6 (NIV)

5But the Lord came down to see the city and the tower the people were building. 6The Lord said, "If as one people speaking the same language they have begun to do this, then nothing they plan to do will be impossible for them."

Even God acknowledges the intelligence of His creation, Mankind, so, again, no one is questioning the intelligence of God's creation; but we need to grasp the intensity of that statement: *Nothing they plan to do will be impossible for them.* With this statement, God decided to confuse the languages and scatter the people about the earth. Why would He do that? He created us, I'm sure He knew how intelligent we were as a people. Human intelligence did not in any way come as a surprise to God; this was merely an acknowledgement of an already established truth – Mankind is made up of intelligent beings. The thing is intelligence does not translate to Wisdom and/or Understanding. Wisdom and Understanding has to do with God and our relation to Him while intelligence does not necessarily have anything to do with our understanding of God. In truth, I can argue that intelligence indeed has something to do with God because intelligence has to do with our understanding of the world and the laws that govern the world in which we live and God created it all. So in a sense intelligence can be seen as an attempt to understand God through His creations and the laws He established to govern them but it doesn't have to be viewed this way. So though an argument can be made that even intelligence has to do with God and our relation to Him, I will say that it doesn't have to, at this point. We can have wildly intelligent people who do not believe in God and they may be able to tell us a great many things about the world in which we live but they wouldn't necessarily be able to tell us much about God. They may be intelligent, yes; Wise, not necessarily. In this regard, you will have intelligent people using their understanding of the world to try and explain God which does not make much sense when you think about it. Can you dissect the automobile and grasp from it an understanding of Henry Ford? It certainly sounds foolish to consider understanding all the complexities of the man, himself, Henry Ford – his life, loves and deepest thoughts simply by pulling a part an automobile. Why would one think that by dissecting the world and the laws established to govern it that we can understand God? It is times like this when our intelligence becomes stupidity and our so-called wisdom becomes our downfall.

THIRTEEN:

"The further a society drifts from the truth, the more it will hate those that speak it."

– George Orwell

THE PATTERN OF THIS WORLD

THE MORE I STUDIED Mindset, the more I became aware of how vital it is to our lives. Mindset is hugely important and so much weighs upon it. With the right Mindset, a Christian will follow God anywhere; through the fire – through anything, fearlessly. With the wrong Mindset all it takes is one off day and you come undone; you're looking for the door, shirking your responsibilities and questioning whether He even exists. Mindset is gravely important and we have to make sure we have the right mindset going into our every day. We have to make sure our hearts and minds are fixed on Him, on Truth; otherwise our hearts and minds will be fixed on the lies of our Perceived Realities.

Romans 12:2 (NIV)

[2]Do not conform to the pattern of this world, but be transformed by the renewing of your mind. Then you will be able to test and approve what God's will is – his good, pleasing and perfect will.

One thing we should understand right away from this scripture is that when we conform to the pattern of this world, our minds become corrupted. In order for our minds to be restored, we must change; we must *no longer conform to the pattern of this world.* When we choose to reject the world we are choosing to conform to Godliness and through this we allow our minds to be renewed, prompting true transformation. One huge problem with Christians, today, is that we do not understand this scripture and miss some very important key points.

The first thing we need to understand about this scripture is that it is not talking about our *actions. This scripture is talking about the mind.* If we change our actions but do nothing to change our mindsets we will return to the very actions we are trying to change but if we change our minds – *if we conform to Christ in our minds* – our actions will follow.

The second thing that jumps out is that the onus is *on us* to *no longer conform.* This is our responsibility. This is what God expects you and me to do out of love for Him. He expects us to change. The scripture then says, *but be transformed by the renewing of your mind.* Once again the onus is on us. God wants us to transform and this transformation comes *only* through *the renewing of the mind.*

Now take note that this is the book of Romans. This book was a letter written to the Church in Rome. This is being said to Christians. If you read the book of Romans you will see the amount of sin this particular church was steeped in. God was not merely making a suggestion; He was giving this church the answer to their current problems. They were already Christians but for some reason they were continuing to sin as though they had not yet been set free; as though the blood of Christ had not yet loosed them from the bondage of sin. God was telling them the reason you continue to sin is because you are still Mental Slaves; they were mentally still in their Perceived Realities. God gave them the answer: *you will transform when your minds have been renewed – aligned with Christ; aligned with Truth.* The same holds true for us. Our Mindsets need to be restored to Truth. Our minds need to be restored to that of Christ.

TRUTH SPEAKS

In chapter one, we discussed *Perceived Reality* – an individual's idea of reality based upon *their* perspective and perception. In the subsequent chapters and subchapters, we dissected how our Perceived Realities influence our daily thoughts, actions and attitudes but what we have not done, to this point, is discuss *Actual Reality*.

The simple definition of reality is truth. *Reality* is defined as *the state or quality of being real; the state of things as they actually exist as opposed to an idealistic view of things; the existence of that which is absolute, self-sufficient or objective and not subject to human decisions; truth*. So the short answer, as previously stated, is *truth*. So what is truth?

Truth is defined as *the true or actual state of a matter; a verified or indisputable fact, proposition or principle; having the quality or state of being true; to conform with the facts or to conform with reality*. In short, truth is *reality*. So reality is defined as truth and truth is defined as reality.

Now as we discussed earlier in *We Are All Illusionists*, in Chapter One, there are over seven billion people on the planet each with their own unique perspective on truth. If every single person has their own Perceived Reality that they believe is true then that would mean that there are over seven billion variations of truth to contend with. That could be a little confusing. How would that work? What is truth if everyone's understanding of truth is right to them? That doesn't make much sense, does it? If everyone's version of truth were true our existence would most certainly be the definition of chaos. On the other hand, if everyone's sense of truth is only what is right to them, then in actuality, no one's concept of truth is true. Does that make sense? Truth does not change. Truth is universal. If your truth is only true to you then it is not Truth; it is actually a lie. Do you get it? In order for individual truths or realities to be proven to be true or a lie, there would have to be a

Prime Reality; an *Ultimate Truth.* There has to be a single reality that *supersedes all others by which all others are judged*; there has to be *one truth that exists outside of human perspective so as not to raise one person or people's perspective above another.* Does that make sense? My truth and your truth cannot both be true if we have opposing views but both can be lies. You see, you and I don't have to tell the same lie for us both to be telling lies but if we're telling the Truth, it must be consistent and thus, we would be saying the same thing. Therefore, there can be many variants of lies but there can be only one Truth.

Truth is a constant. Truth is true and remains so regardless of whether you believe it or not. Water has always been H2O – *two hydrogens and oxygen* – even before humanity knew that hydrogen existed. It did not all of a sudden become hydrogen because we discovered hydrogen. God, in His infinite wisdom, set things in motion long before we had the capability to even ascertain the most basic building blocks of Creation. Certainly there are a million sub-atomic levels below the Quark that have yet to be discovered or named and God probably sits back with pleasure watching us squeal with delight as though we *"discovered"* something – something that has been in existence from the moment God said, *"Let there be light!"* What I'm saying is that there are certain laws that have been in existence to govern Creation from the onset of Creation – and probably even from before that. That just makes sense. It also makes sense that since there is one God, there is one version of reality; one version of truth by which all other realities and truths are measured and this reality and truth was present from the very beginning, before we even realized that truth, reality and lies existed.

John 14:6 (KJV)

6Jesus saith unto him, "I am the way and the truth and the life: no man cometh unto the Father but by me."

Jesus is that truth. He said that He is the way and the truth and the life. To put that plainly, what Jesus is saying is that there is no other path than the path He has paved; there is no other truth than that which He speaks and there is no other life than the example that He has left for us. What this means is that anything outside of Jesus is a lie. Any path that deviates from the path of the self-sacrificial love that He exemplified, even if it is only a slight deviation, is a lie. Any understanding that differs from His truth is untrue. Any life that is not lived for God in complete submission to love is death! There are no other options. There is no fence to ride, here. You either follow the path that Jesus paved or you follow one of the many other paths out there that lead to death. It is that simple. Virtually every decision we make is a decision between life and death. We are either making decisions that lead us towards becoming more like Christ or making decisions that continue to allow us to conform to the patterns of this world; we are either becoming more like Jesus or more rebellious to God. *The path to truly becoming like Christ begins with recognizing that "Jesus is Lord" is the most truthful statement that any human being can make and living it every day is what it means to truly be alive.* It brings a whole new sense of understanding to the famous quote: *"Everyone dies; but not everyone truly lives!"* True life is found in Christ alone. Everything else is merely death waiting to happen.

WINESKINS AND WINE

Matthew 9:15-17 (NIV)

15 *Jesus answered, "How can the guests of the bridegroom mourn while he is with them? The time will come when the bridegroom will be taken from them; then they will fast.*

16 *No one sews a patch of unshrunk cloth on an old garment, for the patch will pull away from the garment, making the tear worse.*
17 *Neither do people pour new wine into old wineskins. If they do, the skins will burst; the wine will run out and the wineskins will be ruined. No, they pour new wine into new wineskins and both are preserved."*

The metaphor in this parable was drawn from contemporary culture. When wine is new it is in a state of fermentation – *transformation.* The wine bubbles and expands as the fermentation gases are released. A fresh pliable wineskin can absorb the expansion of the wine and slowly age with it until the fermentation process is complete. Old wineskins would have already stretched to their limit and become brittle. Placing new wine in old wineskins would force the old skins to stretch beyond their limit and eventually burst, destroying the skin and spilling the wine, ruining both. It is virtually impossible to ferment new wine in an old wineskin. Thus, one lesson we can take from this scripture is: *you cannot put new convictions into an old mindset.* We need a new mindset. Our minds must be renewed; they must be purged, baptized; we must change the way we think in order to truly transform into what God desires. As a chain is only as strong as its weakest link, so faith is only as strong as the mindset in which it inhabits. Like new wine bursting the seams of an old wineskin, so the fullness of Spiritual Understanding cannot be contained in the shallow basin of a Worldly Mindset. The world does not understand the mindset of Christ and rejects it. So when we hold on to worldly views and thoughts, it is like we are choosing to fill the room in our hearts and minds that was meant for God with all kinds of junk, limiting our room for God. We are, therefore, limited by our mindset. What you will and will not attempt, pray about, do or even encourage others to do is completely dependent upon your mindset. An old, Worldly Mindset is stretched to its limit already and will burst at the seams as faith is enacted and convictions are poured in. The Worldly Mindset is so full of guck and worldly convictions that lead to death, that there is scarcely any room for the Godly convictions about righteousness and Love to be stored much less have room to grow and blossom. Our mindsets are the wineskins into which conviction is poured and the limitations of these old Worldly Mindsets shows in our daily walk with God. We need new wineskins. We need the transformation that only comes through the renewal of our minds. We need new mindsets. The same old mindsets will only yield the same old results. If we desire true transformation we need to walk the path that allows it to come to fruition. That means we have to make some serious decisions about our lives, the results we've had and the results we seek. In the Academic world, they say that there are two mindsets and neither is better than the other. In the Spiritual world there are two Mindsets as well but that is where the similarities end. In the Spiritual world, the two mindsets are *the Old Wineskin Mentality* and *the New Wineskin Mentality*. Let us take a look at both.

FOURTEEN:

"Progress is impossible without change and those who cannot change their minds cannot change anything."

– George Bernard Shaw

THE OLD WINESKIN MENTALITY

THERE IS A PASSAGE in Matthew 13:54-58, where Jesus returns home to Nazareth and only performs a few miracles. The faith is so lacking in His hometown that it can appear that their lack of faith somehow hindered Jesus. Let's take a look at that passage in the New International Revised Version of the Bible.

Matthew 13:54-58 (NIrV)

54He came to his hometown of Nazareth. There he began
teaching the people in their synagogue. They were amazed.

"Where did this man get this wisdom? Where did he get this
power to do miracles?" they asked. 55"Isn't this the carpenter's son?"
Isn't his mother named Mary? Aren't his brothers James, Joseph,
Simon and Judas? 56Aren't all his sisters with us? Then where did this
man get all these things?" 57They were not pleased with him at all.

But Jesus said to them, "A prophet is not honored in his
hometown. He doesn't receive any honor in his own home."

58He did only a few miracles there because they had no faith.

There are two things I want to point out before we move forward. The first one is obvious but I feel it needs to be stated all the same: *Jesus was not limited in any way because of their lack of faith.* The second thing is: *the people did not see Jesus; they only saw Mary and Joseph's son.* Let me explain . . .

The Greeks, with all their gods, believed that the gods thrived off of faith and so the more you believed in the gods, the greater they became. The converse of this was also true, the less you believed, the weaker they became and if the people together completely denied their existence, the gods would die. In a sense, the immortality of their gods was dependent upon the faith of us mortals. Now this belief has managed to survive throughout the years and though the Greeks are credited for it, the roots of this belief probably goes as far back as the ancient Egyptians and even to the Sumerians before them. For the false gods of Mesopotamia, Egypt, Greece and Rome, any belief they choose to employ is fine but that does not translate over to the God of Creation. God is not lessened in any way by the lack of faith of those who claim to follow Him or the flat out denial of those who do not. It is Jesus who said in Luke 19:40, *"If they keep quiet, the stones will cry out."* The truth will remain even if all of Mankind refuses to admit it. God's existence does not rely on the acknowledgement of Man. He was God before He chose to create Man. Our God is beyond human intellect. The Time Magazine headline that presented the question, *"Is God Dead?"* is grossly ignorant in that the question alone attempts to limit the immortal God of all Creation to the perceived mortality of the false gods. God is God whether we choose to believe in Him or not. Nothing we do or say can diminish that fact.

Once we can accept that God is beyond mortal limitations and not bound by the faith or lack thereof of mortals, it should become clear that Jesus was not limited because of their lack of faith. He could have done more but to what end?

What was the point of miracles? Did Jesus heal people, walk on water and feed thousands with nearly nothing to impress people or was it to draw them nearer to God? What was the purpose of the first miracles in the Bible? In Exodus 4:1-5, God performs miracles for Moses *"so that they may believe that the Lord, the God of their fathers – the God of Abraham, the God of Isaac and the God of Jacob – has appeared to you."* The purpose of the miracles was ultimately to draw the people closer to God; to cause them to believe in something bigger than themselves; to show them wonders and puzzlements; to make them question what is and is not possible.

When Jesus was among the people of His hometown of Nazareth, they were unwilling to see the possibilities that were before them. They were stuck on the notion that they knew Jesus. They couldn't see past what they thought they knew to see what Jesus was trying to show them. In a sense, it became pointless. He could have caused the day to become black as night and they would have still stood around wondering amongst themselves if He wasn't *Joseph's son.*

In Luke 24:13-35, also known as: *On the Road to Emmaus* in the NIV, we see a similar situation unfold. Jesus did not attempt any miracles, here – His presence alone was the miracle! After resurrecting from the dead, Jesus approaches two believers and makes it so that they could not recognize Him. Jesus walked seven miles with them as He explained, as the scriptures say, *everything in the scriptures that concerned him,* before revealing Himself to them. Why didn't Jesus just reveal Himself to them, right away? Was He unable to because of their lack of faith? No; they were kept from recognizing Him because they were *not quite there.* Jesus explained everything in the scriptures that concerned Him as they walked and opened their eyes, which is another way of saying *He raised their level of belief, faith and conviction to a point where they were able to handle the amount of Truth He was prepared to reveal.* All of a sudden, they realized they are walking with the Son of God, Himself and Jesus disappears from their sight! How humbling, terrifying and yet heart-warming that must have been. Jesus cared enough about those two individuals that He explained to them all that concerned Him in the scriptures and He didn't reveal Himself to them until they were at a point where they could handle that *amount of truth.*

Why did Jesus only perform a *few* miracles in His home town? He only performed a few miracles because that was all *they could handle* at that time. It's not that Jesus could not perform more miracles, it's that too much would have blown their minds and may even have been counterproductive; they simply were not ready for what Jesus was prepared to reveal and so they missed out. Think about what you might be missing out on – what *Understanding* God is holding back from you because you have deemed yourself too intelligent to accept the simple things of God. Don't allow your intellect to become your downfall. Don't let what *you think* you know of God, Jesus and the scriptures hinder your heart from growing closer to Him. *Sometimes the Truth is in a whisper; sometimes it is in the storm.*

The reason the townspeople of Nazareth were not ready is, as we stated earlier: *the people didn't see Jesus the Son of God; they only saw Jesus the son of Joseph and Mary.* The people could not accept Jesus for who He was because they could not *see past the past.* They heard of the miraculous events and saw the miracles; they heard the claims that He could be the Messiah but they had difficulty seeing beyond what they thought they already knew. No matter what they saw or heard about Him what they knew for certain was that this was the child that grew up in Nazareth. They saw only the Carpenter and Rabbi; Jesus was Joseph's son, not God's. Their collective mindset was closed to Him being anything more than that. Their faith in Jesus being anything other than the boy they knew all grown up was all but dead. He could have performed dozens of miracles but it would have been to no avail. *They would only accept the amount of truth they were willing to accept and they were not ready for the whole Truth.* They were not ready for Jesus. The same is true for us, today. *We only accept the amount of truth we are willing to accept.* What this means is that if the Truth does not jibe with our sentiment or understanding, we will not accept it. This is why a new Mindset is so necessary. The old Mindset is limited; without change there can be no growth. In order for growth to occur, the Path of Transformation dictates that we begin with a new idea – an opinion. As the opinion takes hold it becomes a belief. The more the belief grows on you it begins to require testing to prove that it is true. Faith begins as we live out the belief. As God confirms our faith, conviction is created. As conviction becomes cemented within us it creates a Mindset shift – what I like to refer to as *the rewriting of our DNA.* The conviction becomes immovable and we begin to manifest actions spurned by those new convictions. Because we only accept the amount of Truth we are willing to accept, the whole process can get snagged simply because we don't believe something is possible. For this reason, God often takes baby steps with us in initiating the beliefs that lead to transformation. In order for them to truly see Jesus, they would have had to have been willing to see past what they knew and step into faith; they had to step out of their comfort zone and for those people, at that time, that was too much to ask.

The people of Nazareth represent the Old Wineskin Mentality. What this translates to today are people *with a form of Godliness but denying its power* (2 Timothy3:1-5). The Old Wineskin Mentality is the mentality of people who call themselves Christians but they have certain characteristics that are counterproductive to the Christian faith. In essence, *they are still worldly.* They can tend to be people who are not teachable, pliable or moldable and if they are, they are only teachable to a point. They tend to have preconceived notions, expectations and understandings that are non-negotiable not because scripture says so but because *they feel so*; feelings can tend to override scripture on matters that mean a lot to the individual. For instance, a Christian may say, *"I hate homosexuality"* but won't feel as strongly about their use of profanity. They may brandish picket signs that speak derogatively of homosexuals yet show support of or idolize a racist or a man who cheats repeatedly on his wife or a cutthroat, cheat of a businessman because he is *"successful"*; they are willing to forgive the sins of the one yet condemn the other because of their sins. They do not see Jesus for who He is, they see Jesus for *who they think He is* or *who they think He should be*; they can tend to have a *"God is on my side"* view of the world, rather than a *"I am on God's side"* mentality; they will have a user-friendly relationship with God – we're friends as long as your doctrine fits my agenda. This usually results in bottling Jesus up within the confines of their mindset rather than unleashing themselves in His. They are often followers with a *"weak god"* complex; which usually means anything that they can't explain or fathom simply cannot be done and so God becomes trapped within the laws of their logic or what they read in a Science book. They often flip-flop on debatable topics or simply claim many different positions – which translates to a lack of any real conviction. God is not bigger than their problems or circumstances so they pray as a matter of course – *because I'm supposed to* – not because they actually expect to see God work in their lives. When He does work in their lives, they're shocked and awestruck and often try to explain it away because deep down they didn't really expect much. Faith may be present but very little. Their lack of faith tends to make them extremely self-reliant. The *"talented"* or *"sharp"* people can seem to thrive within the Old Wineskin Mentality because they can easily mask their lack of faith and heart with talent or flare. They despise or ostracize those who can see through their façade out of fear of being found out. They gravitate towards excuses when it comes to their own shortcomings and will quench the spirit and faith of others who challenge them with their lives. Because they don't have the same level of faith or heart they will try to stymie yours in an attempt to fit you into the same box they are stuck in. Within the Old Wineskin Mentality are Christians who are less about God and more about the individual. They tend to focus more on being friends than a God-centered relationship. They might fight tooth and nail in favor of the idea of being slaves to sin after salvation because it allows them a viable reason to remain the same or only change the things they want to change and continue to hide or suppress the things they don't really want removed from their lives. It allows the perfect excuse for remaining in sin; especially when it comes to the sins they have fallen in love with.

I can go on about the Old Wineskin Mentality and all the characteristics therein but I simply do not have the time or the room to do so. No matter how many I list, I am sure I will miss some. Every individual does not have to encompass all of these examples but every individual will definitely possess some of them; even if it is only one or two.

The most important thing to take away about the Old Wineskin Mentality is that it is limiting in nature. The Old Wineskin Mentality is all about creating walls within which the Christian is locked in an attempt to render them ineffective. This alone should be the biggest tell-tale sign that your mind is still trapped within a Perceived Reality; though it may be a slightly different Reality than the one you had prior to coming to the Lord, it is a mental trap all the same, designed to keep you from the true freedom that is found in Christ.

THE NEW WINESKIN MENTALITY

In the Old Wineskin Mentality, the growth of conviction is limited because faith is limited. In the New Wineskin Mentality, the doors of faith are blown completely off their hinges! Let's look at one example of this in the scriptures.

Mark 9:17-24 (NIV)

17 A man in the crowd answered, "Teacher, I brought you my
son, who is possessed by a spirit that has robbed him of speech.
18 Whenever it seizes him, it throws him to the ground. He foams at the
mouth, gnashes his teeth and becomes rigid. I asked your disciples to
drive out the spirit, but they could not."

19 "You unbelieving generation," Jesus replied, "how long shall I
stay with you? How long shall I put up with you? Bring the boy to me."

20 So they brought him. When the spirit saw Jesus, it
immediately threw the boy into a convulsion. He fell to the ground and
rolled around, foaming at the mouth. 21 Jesus asked the boy's father,
"How long has he been like this?"

"From childhood, he answered. 22 It has often thrown him into
fire or water to kill him. But if you can do anything, take pity on us and
help us."

23 "If you can?" said Jesus. "Everything is possible for the one
who believes."

[24]Immediately the boy's father exclaimed, "I do believe; help me overcome my unbelief!"

Jesus goes on to cast out the evil spirit and heal the man's son. This is an amazing passage but the focal point here, isn't so much what Jesus did as it is what the boy's father said. He brought the boy to Jesus and His disciples could not toss out the evil spirit. For this man, bringing his boy to Jesus was a display of faith. He believed that the boy would be healed but when the disciples could not cast this spirit out, reality began to set in – perhaps I should say: *'Perceived Reality'* began to set in. I am sure the man's heart fell at the possibility that his son would not be healed. I have a child with a disability. I know what it's like to have doctors give you a prognosis you're not ready to hear. I know what it's like to watch your child suffer, your wife cry and feel utterly helpless, knowing that you can do nothing to change their situation. I know what it's like to hope for your child and I know how crushing a blow to your faith it can be when in your moment of hope the bleakness of reality sets in. I don't have to imagine what it must have felt like to watch the disciples fail and all of a sudden the possibility of your son getting better begins to slip away. I understand completely when the boy's father turned to Jesus and said, *"If you can?"* His walls were going up. The light at the end of the tunnel was all but gone; darkness was closing in on him from all sides. Hope was all but lost then Jesus tells him, *"Everything is possible for him who believes."* That statement was a veiled question. It is a question that every one of us must face and answer for ourselves. The question is not simply, do you believe as much as it is *what do you believe about me?* Jesus is asking, *"Who am I to you?"* Most Christians would answer: *the Son of God.* And you would certainly be correct in saying that but what does that mean to you? How does that knowledge affect your life? In other words, what I'm saying is *so what if He's the Son of God if the knowledge of this does nothing to change you.*

You see, Jesus said, *"Everything is possible for him who believes."* That's a pretty telling statement, isn't it? Everything is possible for him who believes. I want you to think about that statement for a moment and then consider this: *Do you believe in God?* Most people would say yes. Certainly the Christians would answer with a resounding, *"Yes!"* Is everything possible in your life? Silence! If your answer is anything other than YES then Jesus is saying, *"Then you don't really believe."* Do you see that? That's pretty intense! It's kind of like a mathematical equation *(EP=B).* Everything is Possible is the result of Believing that Jesus is the Son of God. So according to the Son, if you believe He is who He says He is, for you, *everything is possible.* The statement remains true when you negate it, too. *If everything is not possible, then you do not believe.*

So the question needs to be asked, then, is EVERYTHING POSSIBLE for you? Is everything possible FOR YOU? It either is or it is not. You either believe Jesus is the Son of God and you believe everything is possible or you do not believe that everything is possible which means, you do not believe that He is the Son of God. Either everything is possible or you do not truly believe. Either everything is possible or you truly believe the lies over the Truth. Do you see that? You can't have it both ways. You can't believe that Jesus is the Son of God and believe that only some things are possible but not everything. Either the statement Jesus made is true or He is a liar; if you say you believe, either everything is possible or *you* are a liar. This is where the proverbial *Excrement* hits the fan.

According to your life, who is Jesus – a liar or the Son of God? Either everything is possible in your life or it's all a lie; that is what it comes down to. This is the scary part – it's not about what you say but about what your life is expressing to the world. You may say that you believe but is your life evidence of that belief? Is *"everything is possible"* evident in your life? *Is your life saying that Jesus is the Son of God and all things are possible through Him or is your life calling the Son of God a liar?*

Faced with this realization, what else could the boy's father say but, *"I believe, help me overcome my unbelief!"*

The New Wineskin Mentality or the Jesus Mindset is about accepting and living according to the understanding that God is great and in Him *all things are possible.* It's about living and walking in faith everyday – pushing the envelope with your life and deepening your convictions to depths beyond your imagination. The Jesus Mindset is about breaking free from your Perceived Reality; free from the mentality of limitations.

That's it. Full stop! There isn't anything more that needs to be said on that. There are no caveats in place to let you *or me* off the hook. The New Wineskin Mentality, the Jesus Mindset, is about stretching you beyond your own understanding because that is what it truly means to walk in faith.

ALL THINGS ARE POSSIBLE

We need to stop limiting what God can do and start acknowledging that *in Him all things are possible.* ALL THINGS ARE POSSIBLE! There is so much more room for growth but we will never get there as long as we reside in a limiting mindset that attempts to fit God in the box of our understanding. In Him the rules of Science do not apply. There is no gravity, physics and the like; there are no laws that can bind Him because it is He who established the laws. There is God and in His reality all things are as He wills from beginning to end. He speaks and it is so. We need to stop trying to fit God in the Realm of Men and begin to truly understand what it means to walk in faith. He is God! He is the Holy One of Israel! It is not God we limit with our Old Wineskin Mentalities, *it is ourselves.*

Help me overcome my unbelief is the prayer of a man drowning in doubt but a man that understands that God can *overcome his doubt.* That should be our prayer every day. Is that something you are asking of God? We need to stop and think about that.

Everything was possible for Jesus and it continually played out in His life. If the same is not playing out in our lives, we need to stop and ask ourselves, who are we really following? Whose children are we? The boy's father was a man of faith who realized that his belief, faith and convictions were *dependent upon circumstances rather than God.* Here is a man that came face to face with the limitations of the Old Wineskin Mentality. It was about to swallow him up until Jesus entered his life. When our belief, faith and convictions are bound to God circumstances don't matter. Circumstances change; God never changes. Are you bound to the Rock or are you bound to your circumstances? Whose child are you?

The Jesus Mindset accepts that there is a vast territory of uncharted faith and there is a willingness to explore it; a willingness to grow beyond our perceived limitations and even beyond your own personal *Realm of Understanding. "Help me with my unbelief"* is asking God to take you beyond your limitations! It is to ask God to take you on a journey beyond your present level of Understanding. We need to stop being so certain about what we think we know about God and allow God to set our thinking straight; to renew a right spirit within us; to renew our mindset. Through Him we can become *truly free.* Freedom in Christ is not about doing whatever you want to do; we've always possessed the ability to do that. *Freedom in Christ means that you are free to explore the boundless territories that exist beyond your Perceived Reality.* Freedom in Christ is about breaking free from the limitations of Mental Slavery and diving headlong into Truth and wading in the waters of love.

At this point, we all have limited faith. We all exhibit faithlessness at times but through the Jesus Mindset we understand that God exists outside of our limitations and He is more than willing to throw open the floodgates of Truth. We just have to be willing to let go of the Perceived Reality we've held on to for so long. What we must come to understand is *if faith is living out our beliefs, then the difference between doing and not doing is simply a decision.* What will you decide?

FIFTEEN:

"If it is important to you, you will find a way; if it is not you will find an excuse!"

– Anonymous

LESSONS FROM A TAI-CHI MASTER

WHILE AT WORK ONE night, I walked into a Resident's room and caught the tail end of a program he was watching on PBS that featured a Tai-Chi Master speaking to a small audience. He did an experiment with a member of the studio audience, a woman that looked like she could be in her sixties. The Master had her come to the front of the stage and watch him perform a simple move. What he did was stand on one leg and slowly raise the other to waist level and then out to his left side. He then returned the leg to center and then lowered it to the ground. He then asked the woman to perform the move just as he did it. As the woman raised her leg, she rocked so much that she nearly fell over. The Master offered a hand and asked her to try it again. She performed the move – she was a little wobbly but performed the move all the same. The crowd applauded. The Tai-Chi Master asked her to perform the move again. This time he offered only a single finger and the woman performed the move near effortlessly. The audience applauded again. He asked her to perform the move again and once again offered no assistance and the woman began to rock as she did before but she managed to complete the move without falling over. Everyone applauded again and with that, he thanked the woman for her participation and asked her to take a seat. Once seated, the Master asked the audience if they noticed what had just happened. Most people considered it an example of *practice makes perfect*; she seemed to get better with each try except for the last one. That wasn't it. The Tai-Chi Master went on to explain that he certainly could not hold up her body weight with a single finger and even when he held her hand on the second try, he was not fully supporting her weight. He asked the audience what was the difference between her first attempt, the assisted attempts and her final attempt? The only difference, he informed the audience after taking several answers, *was what she believed.* She believed she was being supported and acted accordingly *(faith).* In other words, he never truly supported her on any of the attempts yet she began to perform the move with increasing dexterity each time because she *believed* he was assisting her. Once she perceived assistance, she was able to perform; once she believed that he was not assisting her, her ability to perform the move dwindled. The difference was not his assistance but *her perception of assistance.* As far as he was concerned, he never assisted her once. As far as she was concerned, only the first and final attempts were unassisted. The Master performed this demonstration to illustrate two things to the audience: 1) *that every one of them has ability beyond their perceived limitations. Each member of the audience is capable of far more than they realize or readily achieve because they believe in their limitations.* 2) *This potential – this ability goes dormant and remains unrealized in most people because they do not realize the potential they have. They do not realize what is already inside of them.* Each member of the audience subconsciously raised walls to inhibit their God-given ability because of what they have chosen to believe about themselves.

There is an old Jamaican axom that goes like this: *Belief kills and belief cures!* What this means is that whatever you believe, apply faith to and accept as conviction in your life, has the potential to enslave you or set you free; to kill you or cure you. It's funny when you think about it because what it is actually saying is that you are already free but *depending upon the system of beliefs you choose to employ* in your life, you will either become a slave or come to realize the freedom that is already yours.

The Tai-Chi Master did not ask for a volunteer from the audience. Instead, he walked through the audience saying he needed a volunteer – setting in the minds of the audience that someone would be *chosen* to stand in front of everyone else and *"do something"*. Those that did not raise their hands were already unnerved simply at the prospect of being chosen. Knowing that those who did not volunteer were already raising walls of doubt and imprisoning themselves deeper within their minds, he made sure and chose a woman of this caliber to further emphasize his point. To add insult to injury he chose a woman that was a little heavier than the *"standard"* body-type. The minute he chose her, he could see her face redden and her shoulders slump. This wasn't simply a matter of doubt; her mental inability went so deep that before she even knew what she was being asked to do she was completely convinced that she was incapable of performing. Before she even had the opportunity to try, fear and doubt seized her and left her dead in the water because she immediately saw the impossibility of whatever he would ask and convinced herself that no matter how simple a task was asked of her, she would not be able to do it. The moment he offered assistance, no matter how much or how little he actually offered, she grasped at it because she had more faith *in his skill than her own.* Her doubt made it impossible to perform but the moment she perceived assistance, her doubt was removed and she was able to perform effortlessly. In her mind she relied completely upon the assistance of another while in reality, she did it by herself every time. What this means is that the ability was always in her but doubt and fear crippled her – her mindset made it so that she could not perform.

So what does a Tai-Chi Master teaching a lesson on PBS have to do with Christianity? Everything! You and I are just like those members of the studio audience, crippled by faith in things that are simply not true. God created *you* –a magnificent being full of boundless potential. The potential you have is beyond your understanding at this point but know that God created you that way because it pleased Him to do so; He created all of us that way. His vision for your life surpasses your own but because of fear and learned limitations we often settle for less. Why should we? Why do we? Why live within walls of limitations when there is so much more awaiting you? There is a lot more to you than you realize.

THE 4TH WATCH OF THE NIGHT

Have you ever wondered why Jesus chose to walk on the water? I have a way of wondering about a lot of things when it comes to the scriptures which usually leads me to some deep and intense studies. It was actually this question that started me down the path to writing this book. I remember asking many people why they thought Jesus walked on the water as a young man and I was never satisfied with the answers I received. I get it now. I think as a child I was looking for a deeper answer than the most obvious, easy answer. Jesus walked on the water simply because *He could.*

Matthew 14:22-27 (NIV 84)

22Immediately Jesus made the disciples get into the boat and go on ahead of him to the other side, while he dismissed the crowd. 23After he had dismissed them, he went up on a mountainside by himself to pray. When evening came, he was there alone, 24but the boat was already a considerable distance from land, buffeted by the waves because the wind was against it.

25During the fourth watch of the night Jesus went out to them, walking on the lake. 26When the disciples saw him walking on the lake, they were terrified. "It's a ghost," they said, and cried out in fear.

27But Jesus immediately said to them: "Take courage! It is I. Don't be afraid."

Here is another account of this miraculous event as told in the book of John:

John 6:18-22 (NIV)

18*A strong wind was blowing and the waters grew rough.*
19*When they had rowed about three or four miles, they saw Jesus approaching the boat, walking on the water; and they were frightened.*
20*But he said to them, "It is I; don't be afraid."* 21*Then they were willing to take him into the boat, and immediately the boat reached shore where they were heading.*

22*The next day the crowd that had stayed on the opposite shore of the lake realized that only one boat had been there, and that Jesus had not entered it with his disciples, but that they had gone away alone.*

This was no random act. It's not like Jesus miscalculated and suddenly realized He was left alone on the shore without a boat and decided to walk across the lake. Jesus did this because it was a part of His plan. Jesus sent the disciples ahead of Him in the only boat left on the shore. He dismissed the crowd and then went to pray, allowing the disciples ample time to get far enough out on the lake that no one could mistake the miracle for Jesus walking on an isthmus or something like that. Furthermore, the scriptures say that the wind was against them and the boat was *buffeted by waves*. Not to say that walking on calm water would somehow diminish the miracle but to paint the picture accurately, we have to consider all that transpired. He was walking on rough waters that tossed the boat about. This was as chaotic a time as there ever was on this lake and Jesus walked calmly across the water *for three to four miles*! In the other account in the book of Mark, Mark 6:48, it says that Jesus was about to walk by the boat when the disciples saw Him and became afraid. They thought they were seeing a ghost! It is probably safe to say that Jesus was having a little fun with them, at this point.

The question remains though, why walk on the water? What was it that He was trying to accomplish by doing this?

EMBRACING THE UNKNOWN

A second miracle took place the night Jesus walked on the water. A second miracle occurred that can easily be overlooked because in the eyes of most, it ended in failure. Peter stepped out of the boat and walked on water toward Jesus. Eventually, the reality of what he was doing sunk in and after a few steps, he began to sink into the water . . . but for a moment he walked just like Jesus across the surface of the waters.

Most times we discuss this passage of scripture the focus is on Peter's failure: *he walked but he sank.* The bigger point, in my opinion, is why did Peter walk in the first place? Why did Peter step out of the boat? *I believe the answer is simply because Peter trusted Jesus more than he trusted his own understanding of what is and is not possible.* In Jesus, Peter found *absolute truth*. How about you?

Like the woman who trusted the Tai-Chi Master's ability over her own, Peter trusted Jesus' understanding over his own and walked on water because of it. When Jesus said, *"Come"* I am sure that Peter knew that what he was about to do was impossible by human standards. I am certain that a cold shiver must have run up his spine as his foot touched the water and did not pass through it. His heart must have burned within him! Prior to seeing Jesus walk on the water, Peter would never have considered it a possibility but that was where his faith was; that was the extent of his understanding. When Jesus said, *"Come"*, Jesus invited Peter to step beyond the limitations of his understanding. Peter looked in Jesus' eyes and must have thought: *if you believe, so do I.* That's kind of like that *"I believe; help me with my unbelief"* line, isn't it? It's a similar mentality. It says, *"I'm not there but I'm willing to trust you on this."* This is the definition of being faithful; the definition of being full of faith. Faithful living should stretch you. It should force you to grow beyond the limitations of what you consider reasonable; being stretched beyond what makes sense to you. Peter must have looked out on the waters and thought, *"This is crazy! But I believe."* He applied faith as he stepped out of the boat and walked towards Jesus.

When's the last time you thought, *"This is crazy! But I believe"?* When is the last time your faith frightened you? When is the last time your faith in God stretched your understanding? Jesus stretched the understanding of His followers and called them to faithfully follow. If He's not stretching your understanding you need to soberly consider whether you are faithfully following Jesus or sitting on the sidelines enjoying the view.

Do you trust your understanding in the hands of Jesus? Do you trust Jesus with your life? Do you trust Him enough to walk faithfully? Would you have trusted Jesus enough to have stepped out of the boat? Many might think so; I know I always did but the answer to that question is simple: *are you stepping out of the boat, now?* If you're not stepping out of the boat now you wouldn't have stepped out of it, then. If you're not pushing the boundaries of your understanding and faithfully following Jesus into the unknown then you would have sat in the boat with the other disciples and *watched Peter walk on the water.*

Discipleship should be radical, not tame; not subdued. We need to be those who are fanning into flame the Spirit within rather than quenching it with our fears and perceived limitations.

BABY GAP

Bold faith creates deep convictions and bold faith is created when an understanding that goes beyond the norm or beyond common sense is challenged. Our understanding should challenge us to walk in faith. And our faithful walk should challenge others to deepen their understanding and walk in their own faith. I am going to share an example from my life of faith that challenged my wife and I and inadvertently challenged others as well.

In early 2000 my wife and I relocated to Connecticut from New York. My sister was attending school at Wesleyan University in

Middletown, Connecticut, so we got to spend a lot of time together and when summer came, she returned to New York and found a summer job in Manhattan. She was working at the Baby Gap in the mall inside of the World Financial Center. Although we were living in Connecticut, my wife held onto her job in New York City because, as crazy as it sounds – *and this is 100% true* – her commute to work was actually a half hour shorter coming from Connecticut than it was coming from Queens, New York. Seriously! Anyway, we became pregnant with our first child that summer and since my sister was working for Baby Gap, we decided to stop in. Apparently there was a huge End-of-Season Sale going on and she had an Employee Discount to add to that.

As most couples do when they are pregnant with their first child, we did not make an official announcement until we passed the three month mark but we did let immediate family know ahead of time. We had been praying for our children-to-be for quite some time so once we knew we were pregnant, we were pretty excited. Some would even say we jumped the gun a little bit – we told our families that we were pregnant within the first week after conception. We had no official confirmation and didn't even check an Early Pregnancy Test. We didn't need to, we just knew. We were married seven years before we tried to get pregnant and I think we discussed baby names on our honeymoon, if not before getting hitched. We prayed not just for our first born but for all three of the children we planned on having and we prayed for each one specifically – by name. We didn't need an E.P.T. to know we were pregnant; I think God set one in our hearts. When we finally did go to the doctor it was to confirm what we already knew.

It was August or early September when my sister told us that Baby Gap was about to have their annual End of Season Sale where you can get clothes with deep discounts. On top of that, she had an Employee Discount that would lower the prices even more. Without hesitation, we headed down to New York and racked up a bill that totaled somewhere around four hundred dollars after the discounts, on clothes ranging from infant all the way up to 5T – and for good measure, we threw in a few items up to size 7. We bought *all boys clothing.*

As we waited on line, a couple came up behind us and took note of the cart full of clothes. They asked if we were shopping for a family member because we didn't exactly look like we were pregnant; Yasmin wasn't showing much at all. We told them that we were shopping for our baby and Yasmin rubbed her tummy and told them that she was about two months pregnant. The wife, who looked uncomfortably overdue, laughed and said, *"Boy, you must really be excited about it. Obviously your first, right?"* We laughed right along with them and told them he indeed was our first. That comment did not go unnoticed. The husband assessed our cart and asked how we could possibly know the sex of our child if we were only two months pregnant. We told them that we prayed for a boy. Actually, we prayed for all three of the children we wanted – boy, girl, boy. He was taken aback and shook his head as he said, *"For your sake, I hope you do have a boy."* We all laughed at that.

We waited the standard three months before giving our official announcement to friends and extended family. Along with the official announcement, we let everyone know that we were having a boy. We explained to everyone as we informed them that we prayed for a boy. It all seemed pretty simple, to us. Apparently, it was not at all so simple to others. I had no idea the response our announcement would bring. An Elder's wife whom we'd known for years actually pulled Yasmin aside and told her that she was setting herself up for failure. She said that we shouldn't announce the sex of the child until it was confirmed by the physician. Yasmin was perplexed. She was told that announcing that we were going to have a boy when we did not know for certain was prideful and that we were almost tempting fate. We didn't see it that way and Yasmin told her that pride had nothing to do with asking God for a boy and faithfully waiting with eager expectation for that boy to arrive – *that's actually the definition of faith.* She was asked how she would respond if we had a girl, would we be embarrassed or even possibly become angry with God? Looking back, I can understand where she was coming from. She was trying to protect our faith. The thing is we didn't see the harm in *being faithful*; only the hope in receiving an answered prayer. Yasmin answered something along the lines of: *"Why would I be upset if God chose to give us a girl? We have a new child. Our first child! I will be grateful for whatever God chooses to give us but that doesn't mean that I'm going to be faithless about what we asked for in prayer. We asked for a boy and until a girl is born and confirmed by the delivering doctor, we will continue to believe that we are going to have a boy – not because we are anything special but because God is God; and this is nothing for Him."* No more was said about it.

We ran into a couple at the Green Acres Mall in Long Island, who told us that they were praying that we would have a girl so that God would humble us. I found that odd and maybe a little disturbing, to be honest.

It was funny how the opposition began to grow as the months slipped by. More and more people began to ask us if we confirmed with the doctor whether we were having a boy or a girl, as if the doctor's word was final. We never asked. We said that we did not need confirmation from the doctor; we would receive the answer to our prayer when our son was born. The more people heard that answer, the more people shook their heads in disbelief. Now, I don't want to make it sound like there were only naysayers around us because that is simply not the case. There were a few people who were in our corner and encouraged us. There were a few who were eagerly waiting for our son's arrival as though it was their own child.

My parents came to one of our final appointments and the doctor wrote our babies sex down on a piece of paper and showed it to them and then tossed the paper after asking us one final time if we wanted to know. Our OB/GYN was a Believer and was among the few who encouraged our faith. We both said no and she smiled. The funniest part is after we exited the office, I realized I left my Thermos in the exam room and went back in to retrieve it. I grabbed my Thermos and stopped in the doorway looking back at the small waste paper basket on the opposite side of the room. The amount of temptation that weighed upon me to take a look at the piece of paper from the trash and find out what the doctor wrote down was insane! I remember hesitating, standing there a few clicks before finally whispering a prayer and walking out.

In March our son, Magnus-Storm, was born.

Sometimes it is the people closest to you that test your faith the most. The funny thing is that we didn't even see it as *faith* until people began to oppose the possibility of our having a boy. It seemed silly to us. It wasn't like there were a host of options before us. The baby would be either a boy or a girl. We were simply asking God to lean a bit more on one side than the other. Once we did begin to see it as a faith issue, the more opposition arose, the deeper we dug our heels in.

I remember holding my breath at the moment of his birth. For a brief moment, as I encouraged Yasmin to push and held her hand that thought ran through my mind: *what if it is a girl?* I immediately pushed it out of my head and focused on Yasmin and the delivery of my first born. Once he was born, none of it seemed to matter anymore. God gave us a child. God gave us a special gift that we would be responsible for the rest of our lives – a blessing.

Boy or girl? We never really considered that to be a grand stretch of God's abilities. We still don't. *Boy or girl was in God's realm; our realm simply consisted of asking and being faithful.* We prayed for something specific and God answered. Praise Him for that. In the years to come, Yasmin and I had two more children, bringing us to a grand total of three, Summer-Sky and Anniston-Earl – *boy, girl, boy* – just as we prayed and asked God for in the beginning; with the names we chose for them in advance. God gave us exactly what we asked for, not because of anything we did but because it pleased Him to do so and it encouraged us and I'm hoping it encourages you, as well.

GLIMPSING GLORY

Aside from Peter's decision to trust Jesus' understanding over his own, there is another reason Peter ventured out onto the water: *Jesus did it first.* One thing Jesus always did was exemplify whatever it was He asked of His disciples. He never asked them to do things He was unwilling to do – the sign of a true leader. Even though Jesus never sinned, He was baptized by John, a clear sign to us of the importance He placed on baptism. How important should it be to us who have sinned? Jesus had conversations with people everywhere He went and not just for the sake of conversation; He went deep with people and reached their hearts. He told people to come and follow Him and didn't accept their excuses nor did He make excuses for them; He simply placed before each person a choice and then allowed them to stand by their decision. Not everyone followed Jesus but everyone walked away affected by having been in His presence.

If Jesus was standing in the boat and told Peter to step out on to the water, knowing how crazy Peter was, I think he still may have attempted it – he may have hesitated a bit but I think Peter would have given it a try; that's just the kind of person he was. The difference is there would have probably been a lot less faith behind his steps. He probably wouldn't have walked at all. He may have stepped out of the boat and sank into the water immediately. The fact remains, though, that Jesus wasn't standing in the boat; Jesus was standing on the water as though it were dry land having a conversation with Peter after having walked several miles on the water to catch up to the boat. Jesus didn't ask Peter to do the impossible without having first exemplified it for him. Jesus modeled what He wanted Peter to do and then asked him to believe, have faith and allow his faith to mature into conviction.

Jesus exemplified the conviction that He asked of Peter and *expected no less of Peter than what He expected of Himself.* This was no accidental occurrence; this was a calculated move on Jesus' part – a move that was designed to broaden their horizon. Jesus raised their awareness, expanded their worlds, opened their hearts and minds, stretched their understanding – He gave each one of them a glimpse of glory and introduced them to a brand new way of thinking, loving and interacting with the world. In that moment Jesus transformed everything they thought they knew about Him, the world and even themselves. *Jesus walking on the water was less about walking on the water as it was about the unveiling of the New Wineskin into which each one of them could pour faith.* Jesus was not simply walking on the water; *with each and every step Jesus was introducing them to His Mindset, to His perspective, to His Truth.* With every step Jesus showed them that *even in the flesh, all things are possible.* As He walked on the rolling waters, Jesus offered them a glimpse of the world as He sees it – *the way it always has been; the way it is and the way it will remain* – with all things at His feet.

SIXTEEN:

"Change the way you think and you will change the world!"

– Anonymous

FREE INDEED

THE FOLLOWING SENTENCE MAY be one of the most important statements in this entire book. If you come to a deep conviction about what I am about to say, I guarantee that you will be able to overcome just about anything in life – any trap of the mind or body. This is what every Christian must make a conviction and it can and will absolutely transform your life: *The Blood of Christ has set you free!*

I know . . . that doesn't sound like any real revelation. For every Christian this understanding should be a basic piece of knowledge. So I expect some to say: *Yeah, we know that already*. If you are one of those people, you most likely don't understand what I just said. Let me put it this way: *You are already free. As you read this book, right now, if you are in Him, you are free.*

You are free. It is that simple. There isn't some mystical equation or fifteen-point essay answer needed. Christ has already shed His blood and God has already forgiven. You are free. We really don't need any more than that but sometimes we can become so accustomed to captivity that we become afraid and wait for permission to take hold of what is already ours. You are free; *walk in your freedom.* All you have to do is decide to believe that, accept it and make it manifest in your life. It is yours to act upon that freedom or choose to deny it. Should you choose to deny it, you are choosing to remain mentally enslaved. It really is that simple.

Christ's blood has set us free so freedom is ours but some of us choose to remain as we are rather than embrace what we can become. It is like Christ's blood has loosed the chains and knocked the doors from their hinges and knocked every guard unconscious yet we choose to sit in our cells and pine over our captivity. If we choose to remain as we are, are we not rejecting the freedom that His blood purchased as well as the future that His deliverance allows? Are we not choosing to remain a slave? If we do not embrace our freedom it is our fate to watch the future that *could be ours* slip through our hands. It is yours. Believe it. Seize it. Live it. As conviction begins to bloom the transformation you seek will occur.

John 8:35-36 (NIV)

[35]*Now a slave has no permanent place in the family, but a son belongs to it forever.* [36]*So if the Son sets you free, you will be free indeed.*

Jesus tells us, here, that *if the Son sets us free, we are free indeed.* He should know. He is the Son. He is the Son that has set us free with His blood. Jesus died on the cross for our sins, already. Our offenses before God are forgiven and forgotten; they are remembered no more. The blood-debt that we incurred through our rebelliousness was paid in full by Christ on the cross. Through the blood of Christ, we have been set free. We are free! You are free! The Son has set us free, therefore we are *free indeed.* Do you see that? In Christ we are as free as free can be. Jesus never considered Himself a slave to sin and He never allowed sin to get a foothold in His life. One way of looking at it – *and I'm not saying that Jesus thought of it this way, I say this only to make a point* – Jesus considered sin beneath Him. *Why would He willingly defile Himself with sin and mar His relationship with God to please the wants and desires of the flesh? To Jesus, sin was ghastly.* To far too many of us Christians, we consider sin our Master while in the flesh. The scriptures say quite the opposite. We are not just free from the guilt of sin; we are free from the bondage of sin. We are free; free indeed. Who in captivity does not desire freedom but those who utterly deceived?

THE DOUBLE STANDARD

One problem with Christianity today stems from the belief that we remain slaves to sin while in the flesh; whether openly or subliminally, many Christians today hold to this concept. Many churches believe and teach from the pulpits that although we are washed by the blood, somehow that is not enough because we accept the notion that we remain slaves to sin. Believing that we remain slaves after baptism is the mentality of choice because it is simply easier to continue believing that we are slaves than it is to actually consider that we can live up to the calling we have received and simply choose not to. Too few of us wants to come face to face with our sin; too few want to wrestle with their evil desires; that would require too much work and Lord knows the majority of Christendom can't stand the word *"Work".* We want to sit in the hammock of Grace and change nothing. We want to lay back and eat grapes and be fanned by servants like some old Greek painting and point fingers at the heathens for continuing to live in sin. What hypocrites we have become! What is the difference between us and the world if we have no greater expectation for ourselves than sin? We consider *less than the next man* a victory but that was never the standard. That very mindset is what Christ condemned in Luke 18:9-14. Jesus is supposed to be the standard. It is His footsteps we are supposed to be following.

Some Christians become infuriated over homosexuality but are not equally disgusted by their own sin; they have no problem struggling with lust day in and day out – and will even make excuses for it by blaming the objects of their desire, saying the other person was dressed too provocatively. Is it really the clothing that someone wears or the lack thereof that draws us to sin or is it the lack of self-control of the individual who lusts? I have had many conversations with guys about lust over the years and I have always said the same thing when the guy tries to use the woman's clothing as an excuse for lust. I tell them that lust takes place in the mind and she can't tell you what to think. I don't care if the woman is wearing three snow suits and a bag over her head, if I want to lust after her, I will. I don't even have to see a woman to lust; I have a pretty vivid imagination. If I want to lust I can create a woman in my mind from scratch and then create an entire story and setting to go along with it. We do not lust because of what others do; we lust because of what we choose to do deep within the well of our hearts. That is it. We have to stop making excuses for ourselves. When the woman was caught in the act of adultery as stated in John 8, do you think they stopped and had her put clothes on before dragging her before Jesus? Did Jesus use her nakedness as an excuse to ogle her and lust? Now, we do not know for sure that she was naked but being that she was caught *in the act of adultery* it is safe to say she was in some state of undress yet Jesus did not use her situation as an excuse to sin. He expected more of Himself. We need to expect more of ourselves. *We are free and we need to start making decisions like the free men and women we are and stop living like the Mental Slaves we once were.* If you are a Disciple of Christ you need to realize that the bars that once encircled you have been removed; the cage is no more; the shackles have fallen from your wrists. There are no guards and no walls – the blood has set you free. *You are free to run like the Siberian Tiger in the wild but only if you choose to believe.*

100% REPENTANCE

How many of us would get married if our spouse, fiancée or significant other told us prior to taking our nuptials that they can't guarantee that they won't cheat – as a matter of fact, they can most certainly guarantee that *they will cheat*; the question is when and how many times? How many of us would go through with the nuptials at that point? How many of us would hire someone who told us during the interview that he or she intends to embezzle as much as humanly possible? No one would hire that person, right? I mean, I'd give him points for honesty but that's about it – there's no job here for you. No one would truly consider marriage knowing that their potential spouse is *guaranteed* to be unfaithful much less be *unfaithful many, many times.* That just isn't going to happen. Now, are any of these things possible? Of course, anything is possible. Every single husband and wife, no matter who you are, knows that the potential for adultery exists yet every single husband and wife goes into the marriage expecting one hundred percent faithfulness. If our spouses decide to cheat, do we take it in stride or are we aghast, bursting at the seams with anger and disappointment, hurt beyond belief? We are hurt because we didn't expect it. Do you realize what that means? Do you realize that means that the expectation we have for our spouses is perfection? Think about that. Do you realize that every single husband and wife expects perfection from their spouse? We expect perfection from our spouse but we don't have the same expectation in other areas. Why is that? No one likes to admit this because the moment you do all of a sudden the idea of *perfection becomes real.* Lord knows we Christians have a Love/Hate relationship with that word. We don't like to admit this but it is most certainly true: *we expect perfection from others but we do not want to call it "Perfection" because if we do, we will have to expect the same from ourselves.* Like Adam and Eve in the Garden, we will make every excuse conceivable for our own sin yet condemn others for theirs. We expect 100% repentance from others but when it comes to our own lives, our own sin we want God's grace to be an ever-flowing spring of mercy no matter what we do. We must not forget that all sin is an offense to God; ours included.

Jeremiah 3:6 (KJV)

6The LORD said also unto me in the days of Josiah the king, Hast thou seen that which backsliding Israel hath done? She is gone up upon every high mountain and under every green tree, and there hath played the harlot.

Jeremiah 3:14 (NIV)

14"Return, faithless people," declares the LORD, "for I am your husband. I will choose you – one from a town and two from a clan – and bring you to Zion.

Jeremiah 3:20 (NIV)

[20]*But like a woman unfaithful to her husband, so you, Israel, have been unfaithful to me," declares the LORD.*

God uses marriage as an analogy where He, Himself, is the husband and we, the church, are the bride. When we sin, each and every one of us, it is like taking a husband or bride for yourself and watching them commit adultery not once but over and over again – whoring themselves out for their own pleasure without the slightest concern for you or your feelings then begging for forgiveness when the guilt of their actions catches up with them. Soon as they are forgiven they will be back on the prowl for the next John to defile themselves with. It's almost like the abusers in an abusive relationship. They are always hurting the other individual and apologizing but never meaning it. They beg for forgiveness with tears in their eyes, claiming to love the other, promising they will never do it again and before their tears can dry they hurt their partner again. God is merciful and gracious but that mercy and grace should be met with gratitude. In Jeremiah 3:9, it says that when we sin we become like whores, prostituting ourselves to man-made gods of wood and stone. We can do better than that. God deserves better than that. We need to recommit with a clear understanding of not only who we are committing to but the level of commitment we are capable of. Can you imagine a husband telling his wife that he cheated on her and then say, *"Hey, nobody's perfect"?* Can you imagine the rage that would insight? How do you think God feels when we continually sin and say the very same thing? *"Sorry God, but nobody's perfect."* Does that even sound right? Yet we say it all the time; if not with our mouths, we say it with our hearts and actions when we live with the *expectation* that we will continue to sin day in and day out for the rest of our lives.

If you are free from sin then that means you do not have to do it. To continue to sin once you've been set free is not a matter of being a slave to sin but purely a matter of choice. If you are in Christ, you have been set free. Claim that freedom and you will begin to truly experience living life to the fullest. There is an anonymous quote that goes like this: *Life is about choices. You make a mistake once, it's a mistake. You make the same mistake again, that is a choice!* If we Christians are honest with ourselves, in our lives, *we've made more choices than mistakes*. It is time we take responsibility for our actions and start making *clear-minded decisions*. Does this mean that we will never again struggle with sin? Of course, not. That struggle will be with us for life. We will struggle with sin but we don't have to yield to it. He has set us free. The blood has broken the chains. We are free; free indeed. Whether you choose to sin or not, understand that you are only exercising the freedom that Jesus has given you through the shedding of His blood. Now consider if the sin is worth it.

SEVENTEEN:

"You can only fight the way you practice."

– Miyamoto Musashi

LIVE FREE OR DIE

WHILE DRIVING ONE DAY in Connecticut, my children saw a New Hampshire license plate with the motto etched across the top: *Live free or die.* They asked what it meant and I thought it was taken from the famous Patrick Henry quote, *"Give me liberty or give me death!"* Though the same sentiment is expressed, I later looked it up and found out the quote was from a New Hampshire born Revolutionary War soldier named General John Stark. The entire quote was taken from a toast he was supposed to give at a celebratory function sometime after the war. He fell ill and sent a written toast in his absence on July 31,

1809. The entire quote is, *"Live free or die. Death is not the worst of evils."*

General John Stark was absolutely right, *"Live free or die! Death is not the worst of evils."* This is especially true for the Christian. The Christian who views death as a release from this world and acceptance into eternity with God would consider death nothing to be feared. For such a person, death is a calling home and that is certainly not the worst of evils. In this sense, a fate worse than death, for that Christian, would be to continue living in this world as a Mental Slave; to recognize that Christ's blood has freed you from the bondage of sin yet remain powerless to its hold over you.

We need to take hold of the freedom that God has given us. It is ours. It is our right to possess it and retain it. To allow it to slip through our fingers because of a mentality of slavery is like the Israelites in the desert complaining about being better off as slaves in Egypt. We are free. You are FREE! Sin has no hold over you. How can we live in it any longer? We do not continue to sin because we are slaves to it; on the contrary, we continue to sin because we have convinced ourselves that we will . . . and it's okay. We continue to sin because we are convinced that as long as we are in the flesh, we remain slaves to sin. This is simply not true. *We do not continue to sin because we are slaves; we again make ourselves slaves because we continue to sin.* We sin because we choose to sin. We can resist the urge but we give in to sin because we choose to; because we are trapped in the pattern of sin – *the pattern of this world* – the pattern that we have embedded in our DNA and cultivated over the course of our lives. We sin because it is what we've trained ourselves to do our entire lives. We're addicted to it – but every habit can be broken.

Ephesians 4:22-24 (NIV)

[22]You were taught, with regard to your former way of life, to put off your old self, which is being corrupted by its deceitful desires; [23]to be made new in the attitude of your minds; [24]and to put on the new self, created to be like God in true righteousness and holiness.

God says here that we need to put *off our former selves.* That means the ball is in our court. This is a responsibility left to you and me. He then says that when we do that – *put off our former selves which is being corrupted by the deceitful desires of the flesh* – we will be made new in the *attitude of our minds.* Doesn't that sound eerily close to Romans 12:2 – *do not conform to the pattern of this world but be transformed by the renewing of your mind?* Both scriptures refer to a change in Mindset that occurs when we choose to trust in God's wisdom, His understanding over our own and make changes in our lives accordingly. When we go out on a limb and act faithfully trusting in Him and His ways over our own desires and the patterns of our evil habits, a transformation will occur.

We are called to act, here. God says we were *taught to put off our old self.* Doesn't that mean that God is saying that this is something that we *can* do? Is this not an expectation? It is up to us to put off the old and *put on the new self, created to be like God in TRUE righteousness and holiness.* This is a choice *we* must make. And why wouldn't we want to? I believe deep down we want to but for far too many of us, we just don't believe that it's really possible. That is your

Perceived Reality talking. That doubt comes from a mentally enslaved mindset. Christ's blood purchased our freedom. We are free. We are free to choose to either run free in the wilderness of Love or remain enslaved in our minds. The choice is ours. God knows what we can and cannot do because He created us. If He tells us we can do something then we can. To deny that is simply choosing not to accept the words He has spoken. It is like Satan once again asking, *"Is that really what God said?"* There is nothing new under the sun – God has already told us this. Satan is using the same old tricks he always has and he's reaping the same results.

HOW FAR WILL YOU GO?

Hebrews 12:3-4 (NIV)

[3]Consider him who endured such opposition from sinners, so that you will not grow weary and lose heart. [4]In your struggle against sin, you have not yet resisted to the point of shedding your blood.

Did you notice that God used the word *"Yet"*? Do you realize that by using that one little word God is letting us know that resisting to the point of shedding blood is not only something that we are able to do but it is actually a *very real possibility*? The point of telling someone *"not yet"* is to warn them that if they keep on the path that they are on, it is very likely that *"they will"*.

My wife and I have worked with many couples and we often ask this question when trouble arises: *if you knew this situation would arise before you got married, would you have still decided to get married?* It's a question that attempts to take their minds off of the current situation and momentarily refocus it on happier times. Often enough, the couple will assess their marriage and the problem and realize in light of it all that their current situation is just that – *their current situation.* Obviously, this isn't always the case but this allows them to move forward assessing their marriage from a different mindset than the defensive mindset they both most likely had previously. It's not an end all question by any means but it can definitely get the conversation going. Now, let's use that question in relation to God. *If God told you before you became a Christian that you would have to resist sin to the point of shedding blood in order to be a Christian, would you have become a Christian?* It's enough to really make us stop and think, isn't it? How many of us would be Christians, today, if we knew that we were required to resist sin to the point of shedding blood? *How many of us even believe that this is possible?* Guess what? This line was always in the Bible. The possibility has loomed over each and every one of us since day one. As a matter of fact, Jesus did it for you. Would you be willing to do it for Him?

Many will find this difficult to accept because our will to resist sin is so pitiful that this level of dedication seems unattainable. We give in to sin long before we reach that point; we crumble long before our foundations begin to give way; we fold without ever really looking at our cards because deep down we have accepted failure. We have decided in our hearts that we can't resist, so we give in. This means that you and I do not give in to sin because it is so great and overpowering we give in because we simply believe we have no other choice. Now God isn't saying that we *will have to resist to the point of shedding our blood*, but He is certainly letting us know that we are capable of it. What will you decide in your heart to do the next time you are faced with this decision – resist or give in?

RESIST THE DEVIL

James 4:7 (NIV)

7Submit yourselves, then, to God. Resist the devil, and he will flee from you.

I believe that we, collectively, have not paid enough attention to this scripture. This scripture says that the devil will flee from us if we resist him and submit ourselves to God. Once again, this is a scripture that has always been in the Bible and requires action on our part. *We must submit ourselves to God and we must resist the devil and the worldly desires of the flesh.* God is simply saying if we do those things, Satan will flee from us as one afraid, running with his tail between his legs like a scared puppy. Think about that. We can tend to make Satan out to be this *monstrous being, terrible and horrifying* yet God is saying you have no reason to fear the devil; God is saying that *we have the power. The only power Satan has over us is what we give him.* This means that the power is *ours to give.* That is why he fights so hard to keep us trapped within our *Perceived Realities*; he's afraid that we will learn the truth; the truth he already knows. He is afraid that we will learn that he is powerless. When we choose to sin it is *our choice.* When we choose to resist, that too, is *our choice. He has no power over us!*

How far are you willing to go to resist sin? God is saying that we can resist to the point of shedding blood. We can; we just haven't decided to do that. The point is not that we will but that God is letting us know what is within us. We are stronger than we have come to believe. You are stronger than you think you are. Resist him and watch him cower before you like prey. We truly are lions looking at our reflection, seeing only kittens. We are Navy SEALs who have been deceived into believing we are preschool children with diapers and snotty noses. We are more. You are more. Be more. You *can* resist sin. God says you can. *You have to decide whether you are going to trust the faith He has in you or the doubt you have in yourself.* How far will you go for your God, Father and Savior?

OVERCOMING THE WORLD

This revelation can make us view sin in a whole different way. Once we have been set free through the blood of Christ, we do not continue to sin because we are slaves to sin, we continue to sin because we have developed habits over the years – *a Mindset* of sin that we must overcome through submitting ourselves to God and resisting the devil.

We remain mental slaves of sin simply because we continue to believe we are slaves to sin after salvation and through faith in that belief it becomes manifest in our lives. So when sin occurs it shouldn't be viewed as something we need to continually repent of for the rest of our lives or something we are incapable of ending; it should be viewed as the revelation of a part of our Mindset that still exists in opposition to God and views sin as a justifiable, reasonable option. When we view sin this way, every sin committed is a reminder to us of a part of our hearts that has not yet submitted to God. Every sin is then a reminder of the rebellious parts of our hearts that exist and must be dealt with in order for us to grow deeper in our relationship with God. In a sense, we are involved in situations on a daily basis that has the potential to reveal to us the traps of our mentalities; the deeply embedded sin that we may not even be aware of – not to shove it in our faces but to show us what we already have been set free from. We should praise God for every revelation of sin in our lives whether it comes through friend or foe because we understand it as an opportunity to repent of that sin once and for all. If we are willing to accept it, God has already given us the power to overcome the sin in our lives. We just have to choose to believe it and faithfully live it out every day. Take a look at these scriptures:

I Peter 2:21 (NIV)

21To this you were called, because Christ suffered for you, leaving you an example that you should follow in His steps.

John 16:33 (NIV)

[33]*"I have told you these things, so that in me you may have peace. In this world you will have trouble. But take heart! I have overcome the world."*

I John 5:4-5 (NIV)

[4]*For everyone born of God overcomes the world. This is the victory that has overcome the world, even our faith.* [5]*Who is it that overcomes the world? Only the one who believes that Jesus is the Son of God.*

Do you see what God says in these three scriptures? God says that Jesus left an example that we should follow; we should follow in the steps of Jesus. In John, Jesus says that He has overcome the world. Now without going any further, we should be able to put two and two together, here, and figure out that if Jesus overcame the world and we are following in His steps – *the very path that He was on* – then the very steps we follow *(individually as well as collectively)* is the same path that leads to overcoming the world. This is a simple deduction and the scripture in 1 John puts it all together for us. 1 John tells us that we *have* overcome the world. In Christ, we overcome the world; not future-tense but *right now*. Too often we view this scripture as something that will take place once we've passed on to the next life but God says that He came to give us life to the full – that means right now we can live a full life, enjoying the freedom found in Christ. This very minute as you read this book, understand that if you are in Christ, you have *already* overcome the world. Victory is in the blood. The blood has set you free; you just have to believe this and start making decisions based on this Truth and stop living according to lies. You have overcome the world. That's pretty crystal clear. But let's take this a little further; I want to dispel all doubt, here. Let's look at John, again.

John 8:10-11 (KJV)

10When Jesus had lifted up himself, and saw none but the woman, he said unto her, Woman, where are those, thine accusers? Hath no man condemned thee?

11She said, No man, Lord. And Jesus said unto her, neither do I condemn thee: go, and sin no more.

Following the now famous line where Jesus challenges the Pharisees and Teachers of the Law to cast the first stone if they are without sin – *and they all drop their stones and walk away, Jesus* – who *was without sin and was well within His right to condemn this woman* – forgave her and told her to *"Go, and sin no more!"* That woman's life hung in the balance – Jesus had every right to stone her to death and He told her, *"Go, and sin no more."* What do you think the woman understood when Jesus said that to her? What do you think was her understanding of Jesus' expectation? He could have said 'go and try not to sin too much', couldn't He? If Jesus' expectation was that she would continue sinning day in and day out for the remainder of her life because she was helpless to the sin in her life, wouldn't He have said that? Her life hung in the balance and He chose to say, *"Go and sin no more."* If He didn't expect obedience wouldn't He have said something more along the lines of, *'go and sin less than you did before'* or perhaps, *'how about we try and keep this sinning thing down to a minimum – maybe cut it down a third.'?* Let's not forget that Jesus never sinned. Surely He would understand what it means to *"sin no more"*; He understood what He was asking of her. If His expectations were less than a complete reversal of the sin in her life; turning completely away from sin for good, wouldn't He have said that? Instead, Jesus told the woman to *"sin no more"* and rather than accept Jesus' words, we try to circumnavigate them by convincing ourselves that he didn't mean it like that. *"Is that really what He said?"* Sounds familiar? Satan asked Adam and Eve that same question right before the Fall.

Would Jesus' expectation for this woman be any different than His expectation for us? Think about it honestly, who was this woman? Was she some other worldly being capable of doing the impossible? Might there have been something stamped across her forehead stating: *Aside from this one indiscretion, this woman is fully capable of living sin free?* No, she was a regular woman like any woman you and I would come across, today. The only thing special about this woman is that she was used in a conspiracy to try and trap Jesus. She was caught in the act of adultery. She was a common sinner. She was someone the Pharisees and Teachers of the Law probably thought very little of because they were willing to stone her to death just to prove their point. How many of us have ever wondered what happened to the guy she was caught with?

Why wasn't he dragged before Jesus, as well? If she was caught in the act of adultery then it most likely was the man that she was with who was married – there's no mention of her having a husband. The cheating man was free to go home to his spouse as though nothing had happened – as far as he knew this woman was going to get stoned to death because he engaged her in illicit activity. No one seemed to care for her. In essence, she was considered expendable. And then they brought her before Jesus.

My point is, in the eyes of Men she was a no one. Yet Jesus told her to go and sin no more. She most likely wasn't a practicing Jew and certainly wasn't a Christian, at this point. Yet Jesus told her to sin *"no more"*. Did Jesus have more hope for this woman than He has for you and me? Did He see some hidden potential in her that is absent in us, today? I don't think so. I believe Jesus has the same expectation for us that He had for this woman. He expects us to go and sin no more. He expects us to resist the devil and watch him flee. He expects us to submit ourselves to God. He expects us to live up to the calling we have received.

2 Corinthians 7:11 (NIV)

11See what this godly sorrow has produced in you: what earnestness, what eagerness to clear yourselves, what indignation, what alarm, what longing, what concern, what readiness to see justice done. At every point you have proven yourselves to be innocent in this matter.

What expectation do you truly have for yourself? God says that godly sorrow produces these things within us. Earnestness is motivation produced from deep convictions. Indignation is a righteous anger or disgust for sin. If you have an expectation of sin where would these things come from? What would produce the *"alarm"*, if you expect to sin? When is the last time you were alarmed by your sin; by something you did, said or thought? How could you possibly be *"alarmed"* by something you expect? If there is no earnestness, indignation, alarm, longing, concern and readiness to see justice done can we truly say we have Godly sorrow? If that is the case, what is the alternative? Let's look back at that same chapter and pick it up in the end of verse nine.

2 Corinthians 7:9-10 (NIV)

– Yet now I am happy, not because you were made sorry, but because your sorrow led you to repentance. For you became sorrowful as God intended and so were not harmed in any way by us. 10Godly sorrow brings repentance that leads to salvation and leaves no regret, but worldly sorrow brings death.

The alternative mentioned is worldly sorrow which leads to death. What this means is that worldly sorrow is not repentance at all. Understand that if we have an expectation of sin – *if we continue to consider ourselves slaves to sin while in the flesh; if we believe and continue to live lives that exemplify our powerlessness to sin* – we do not have Godly sorrow as God intends, we only have worldly sorrow which does not truly repent and produces only a form of godliness but denies its power (2 Timothy 3:1-5) – the Old Wineskin Mentality!

SIN NO MORE

When the waters washed over you and the blood of Christ washed away your sins, when the Heavens opened above and the voice of the Father called you His Child, as He did Jesus at the moment of His baptism, when the angels rejoiced in song and praised the Lord for the salvation of your soul, you were set free; free indeed. If you are in Christ, you have been set free. You are no longer a slave to sin. You are free. Go and sin *No More!*

Romans 6:2-14 (NIV)

[2]By no means! We are those who have died to sin; how can we live in it any longer? [3]Or don't you know that all of us who were baptized into Christ Jesus were baptized into his death? [4]We were therefore buried with him through baptism into death in order that, just as Christ was raised from the dead through the glory of the Father, we too may live a new life.

[5]For if we have been united with him in a death like his, we will certainly also be united with him in a resurrection like his. [6]For we know that our old self was crucified with him so that the body ruled by

sin might be done away with that we should no longer be slaves to sin – [7]because anyone who has died has been set free from sin.

[8]Now if we died with Christ, we believe that we will also live with him. [9]For we know that since Christ was raised from the dead, he cannot die again; death no longer has mastery over him. [10]The death that he died, he died to sin once for all; but the life he lives, he lives to God.

[11]In the same way, count yourselves dead to sin but alive to God in Christ Jesus. [12]Therefore do not let sin reign in your mortal body so that you obey its evil desires. [13]Do not offer any part of yourself to sin as an instrument of wickedness, but rather offer yourselves to God as those who have been brought from death to life; and offer every part of yourself to him as an instrument of righteousness. [14]For sin shall no longer be your master, because you are not under the law, but under grace.

We have died to sin. How can we live in it any longer? Count yourselves dead to sin but alive in Christ. How often does a dead man sin? Well, he's dead, so . . .

Do you get the point? Through baptism we not only die with Christ but we are raised to new life with Him, as well. We are free indeed. The old perishes in the waters of baptism and the new rises to life just as Lazarus was called back from death to life by Jesus' command. We are free from the guilt of sin as well as the bondage of sin because through the waters of baptism, God allows us to die with Christ and rise again to new life, just as the scripture says. We, who are born again, born of water and spirit as Jesus commanded, are no longer slaves to sin. We are free!

SLAVES NO MORE

There is no scripture in the Bible that says *you must sin every day for the rest of your life.* I know this is a mind-boggling statement to some but please, check it out. It's not in there.

Romans 6:18 (NIV)

[18]You have been set free from sin and have become slaves to righteousness.

Romans 6:22 (NIV)

[22]But now that you have been set free from sin and have become slaves of God, the benefit you reap leads to holiness, and the result is eternal life.

These scriptures are certainly in the Bible. Scriptures like these reiterates the point that Jesus was expecting the woman to *never sin again* when He told her to, *"go and sin no more"*. Remember Jesus said more than once that He had the power to forgive sins – why would anyone need to be baptized for the forgiveness of their sins while Jesus is standing right there with them? It's kind of like when John the Baptist's disciples questioned Jesus about why His disciples did not fast and Jesus explained to them that there was no need for them to fast because He was with them but when He was gone they would need to fast *(Luke 5:33-39)*. Christ was God in the flesh. There were things that would need to be done when He was gone that was unnecessary when He was right there with them. He forgives the sins of who He chooses as He chooses, just as He did the criminal hanging on the cross beside Him. So this in no way negates or attempts to negate our need for Jesus.

Romans 3:23 (NIV)

[23]For all have sinned and fallen short of the glory of God.

This scripture is still in the Bible and testifies that all of us have fallen and are in need of Jesus. That was never in debate. What is in debate is this Perceived Reality that has rolled over Christendom like a thick fog that blinds and confuses as it tells us that *after coming to the Lord, after He has called us, we are somehow still slaves to sin, allowing most to remain comfortable in their sin even after being washed by the water*. This is a lie from the Devil! God has clearly stated otherwise.

Everything else is just a distraction from the truth. Everything else is just an excuse to sin. We who are in Christ have been set free. You do not have to sin anymore unless you once again allow sin to become your Master by choosing to continue in it. That is not the path of a follower of Christ. We should be different. We should be *in the world but not of the world.* There should be a stark difference between us and those who are not of the Father. It is to our shame when monks, Buddhists and the average Muslim comes across more loving, peaceful and dedicated to their faith than the average Christian.

Genesis 4:7 (NIV)

7*"If you do what is right, will you not be accepted? But if you do not do what is right, sin is crouching at your door; it desires to have you, but you must rule over it."*

Do you realize this was said in the book of Genesis? This was said by God to Adam's son. You would think we would be fully aware of this, today – but most gloss over this scripture as though it isn't scripture; as though God never said it. And this is most likely because most do not understand what God said in this scripture. God said to Cain, *"You. Must. Rule. Over. It."* Do you see that? This means that ruling over the sin in your life is well within the capabilities of Man. It always has been. Now consider that scripture with the scripture we read in the last section taken from Hebrews 12:4 where God says we have not yet resisted sin to the point of shedding blood. Do you see how it all fits together? God is saying that He's given us the ability to rule over the sin in our lives; it is simply a choice but we are unwilling to go as far as we need to go to resist sin. It is within us to resist to the point of shedding blood but we do not because we are simply unwilling. So often we hear people say, *"If it is God's Will"* or *"God willing . . ."* I'm actually tired of hearing that. We need to get off that train and catch the next one. For most of us it is not about what *God Wills* – the question is what is *your will*? God is willing; are you? It is not God's Will that we sin; that is our will. It is God's Will that we *sin no more*. Is that your will? We need to bag the religious-pious-talk and get real with God. Sin put Christ on the cross; do you think God wants us playing tag with it for the remainder of our lives or perhaps skirting as close to it as possible without actually getting burned by it? Is that what He died for? We need to stop feigning humility and start seeking righteousness. It's not about *"God's Will"* if we never strive for anything other than the same old sin we've always been entangled in.

God says we can rule over the sin in our lives. When we continue to yield to sin, are we not with our lives, calling God a liar? We need to hold ourselves to a higher standard and we need to help each other in this endeavor. We need to unite in our struggle against sin; dig deeper and lift one another up when we stumble – encourage and admonish one another and most of all, stand firm, side by side, shoulder to shoulder, heads lifted to the Lord. God believes in us. It is time we awaken the Spirit within as we walk the path that Jesus paved with the same mindset, heart and attitude toward sin. It's time we made the devil run in fear!

God commanded Cain from the very beginning of the Bible to rule over the sin in his life or be ruled by it. Cain decided to give in to his desires. We face the exact decision that faced Cain. We must either rule over the sin in our lives or it will rule over us. What will you choose?

God has already given us the victory. It was ours from the very beginning. We chose to give that power away. Jesus came on the scene to break the cycle of sin and hand us the reigns once again. We are free; free to choose to live for Him or to give in to our desires. We're right back where it all started, let's not be coy about this – let's not make the same decision all over again. The reigns of your life are in your hands. What are you going to do with them?

EIGHTEEN:

"Sometimes people don't want to hear the truth because they don't want their illusions destroyed."

– Nietzsche

TRUE AND PROPER

Romans 12:1 (NIV)

1Therefore, I urge you, brothers and sisters, in view of God's mercy, to offer your bodies as a living sacrifice, holy and pleasing to God – this is your true and proper worship.

That is an incredibly challenging scripture all on its own. I don't think further exposition is at all necessary; the scripture speaks very well for itself but for the sake of being thorough, we're going to take a closer look. Before we get into what the scripture is actually saying let's take a look at another version of the same scripture – this is taken from the New International Reader's Version, an even more simplified version of the scriptures that is primarily geared towards children; it is more or less an easy-reader version.

Romans 12:1 (NIrV)

1Brothers and sisters, God has shown you his mercy. So I am asking you to offer up your bodies to him while you are still alive. Your bodies are a holy sacrifice that is pleasing to God. When you offer your bodies to God, you are worshipping him.

Think about what that says. This is a letter written to the Church in Rome. So this entire letter is written to Christians! This is not written to those who are unaware of their Creator and Father; this is written to those who are supposed to be *"in the know"* – those who are supposed to already be worshipping Him. This is written to those who are supposed to be saved, sanctified and sealed with the Holy Spirit until the Day of Glory arrives and all is revealed and laid bare before the eyes of all of Creation. To those who have accepted redemption through the blood of Christ, God says *sacrificing your body to God is* ***true and proper worship!***

Doesn't this scripture feel like God is attempting to rope in the church in Rome by explaining to them that their mode of worship is inadequate? He is basically saying true worship, proper worship goes deeper than the commitment they had; it's not about sitting in a building on Saturday or Sunday but about the willingness to sacrifice your body, sacrificing your very self to God; *true worship is offering up yourself to God.* This is God speaking to His Children, here; this is God speaking to you and me.

Let me ask a silly question: *How often are you in your body?* We are in our bodies all of the time, right? Our bodies are not things we can put on and take off at our leisure. You and your body are one; there isn't a time that you are not in your body – unless you are in the habit of having out of body experiences. If you are, I'll pray for you. I don't know . . . maybe you are the exception. For everyone else, sacrificing your body to God is not a once in a while thing; it's not a once on Tuesday and twice on Sunday thing. It's not something you take a break from as the urge arises so you can give someone *a piece of your mind.* As long as you are in your body, the expectation remains. If you offer up your body as a sacrifice to God then you are sacrificing yourself; *all that is you is sacrificed to God.* In essence, that means that the sinful you should no longer exist. You are willingly pouring out your wants, needs, desires; your rights, views, political affiliations and aspirations *as a sacrifice to God* because of your love for Him. You are choosing to become *nothing*, without asking anything in return. As John the Baptist said in John 3:30: *He must become greater; I must become less.* This, God says, is *pleasing to Him.* This is true and proper worship: *to empty your life of you for God.*

I'm going to say something that makes me cringe to consider it so I know it will make a few if not all of my readers cringe a little, as well. I am not writing this as someone who has mastered all that this book covers. I write these words as one who honestly believes that God is speaking through me. Believe me, writing this book was not easy for me. I often put the book down for days and weeks at a time in order to wrestle with my own feelings and understanding. So saying this isn't exactly easy for me but I believe it is absolutely true: *If the willing sacrifice of self to God is TRUE and PROPER worship according to God, doesn't that mean that anything short of that is FALSE, improper or a lie – not worship at all?* I don't know about you but it makes me stop and wonder – in over twenty years as a Christian, have I been *truly worshipping God at all?* That's a humbling thought. God is truly patient and Loving.

Have I worshipped God with my all? Have I given Him my best? Was my offering pleasing to the Lord as was Abel's so long ago or was it displeasing and rejected as was Cain's offering? Those are the only two choices; either you are worshipping in Truth which is acceptable or *sin is crouching at the door; it desires to have you but you must overcome it.* Where do you stand? Does God long for us to worship Him in truth or is it that we think He should be satisfied with worship that amounts to nothing more than a lie?

John 4:23-24 (NIV)

[23]"Yet a time is coming and has now come when the true worshippers will worship the Father in the Spirit and in truth, for they are the kind of worshippers the Father seeks. [24]God is Spirit and his worshippers must worship in the Spirit and in truth."

This is Jesus speaking here. Jesus says that the time is coming and has *now come*. This is no prophecy of the future; this was a testament of the times that were at hand. Jesus was talking about His days and the days that would follow as the Spirit ushered in the Age of the Church. If the time to worship God in the Spirit and truth has already come, where is the evidence of it, today? Where are the Christians that worship God as He demands – in Truth, a willing sacrifice of self to the glory of the Father? This will never be preached by the private jet owning, big house and fancy car driving *"ministers"* who do all they do to the glory of self? They preach a ministry of prosperity and worship a genie in a bottle. They do not preach the Truth.

True Christians are out there. The problem is they are not the many but the few. In this world of over seven billion souls, there are several million, if not billion who claim to be Christian. Of that lot, very few are truly worshipping the Father in Spirit and in Truth; it would be evident otherwise. I don't say this to point fingers at others; I say this for us to point fingers at ourselves and ask, *"Am I doing everything that I can to worship Him in Spirit and Truth?"* Lead the way. Be the example. Be the sacrifice. *Let your life be a sermon to others!*

THE EARLY DAYS

Jesus exemplifies everything that is asked of us. So when God defines true and proper worship for us, He is not defining something that cannot be done; on the contrary, He is defining something that has already been modeled for Mankind in Jesus.

Luke 3:21-23 (NIV)

21When all the people were being baptized, Jesus was baptized too. And as he was praying, heaven was opened 22and the Holy Spirit descended on him in bodily form like a dove. And a voice came from heaven: "You are my Son, whom I love; with you I am well pleased."

23Now Jesus himself was about thirty years old when he began his ministry. He was the son, so it was thought, of Joseph, the son of Heli . . .

The scripture goes on from there and details Jesus' lineage all the way back to Adam. As a side note, I just want to say that this passage should be enough to dispel any theory about the book of Genesis – *specifically the first eleven chapters* – being allegory. God, from verse twenty-three onward, goes on to completely derail the entire *Millions of Years Theory* by simply recounting the lineage of Christ backwards from Jesus to Adam. If one chooses to consider the first eleven chapters of Genesis allegory, are you then saying Luke is allegory, as well? If Luke is allegory, what does that then say about the other Gospels? Just a thought; anyway, let's get back to my point. The reason I mention this scripture is that it specifically mentions that Jesus was thirty years old when He was baptized and started His ministry. This is in keeping with

Jewish law at that time. A Rabbi was not able to go out and teach their particular understanding of the scriptures until the age of thirty. The funny thing is similar to today's Christian denominations during the first century there were more than three hundred different interpretations of scripture which varied just slightly one from the other and all had dedicated followers. The two main rabbinical schools at that time were the Houses of Hillel and Schammai. Master Rabbi Hillel was said to be Gamaliel's grandfather – the same Gamaliel who famously warned the Pharisees who were conspiring against Jesus that they may find they are *fighting against God.* The House of Hillel was the prevailing view of the day which contended that tradition was greater than scripture.

There's not much mentioned about Jesus' early days but we know that Jesus was educated as a Rabbi according to ancient Jewish custom. It is generally held that Jesus came up under the tutelage of the House of Hillel, which would have made for some very interesting debates concerning scripture as Jesus held that scripture by far outweighed Jewish tradition and actively opposed that school of thinking. Another interesting piece of information is that from the age of ten to fourteen as a child was schooled in Rabbinical study, they were taught critical thinking through open debates on scripture in the same way a Lawyer is taught Law. Rabbi did not have to seek out followers because they were in such demand that students lined up to be trained under a specific Rabbi whose teachings matched up with their own beliefs. On the rare occasion a Rabbi who was greatly impressed by a Talmid or Rabbinical student's knowledge and handle of the scriptures would seek out the individual for further study. It would make sense that if Jesus truly was trained under the House of Hillel it may be due to his impressive debate with Rabbi and Teachers of the Law at the age of twelve. Hillel or Gamaliel, who may have been present, would have been so impressed with Jesus that they sought Him out as a student.

Either way, what we know of Jesus' youth is that He was a carpenter. Again, it was general tradition that a young man was trained in his father's trade as they attended rabbinical school and by the age of fourteen their path would be clear whether they would continue on in their education and seek out a Rabbi or enter their father's trade professionally. According to many sources, even as the youth were further educated by their chosen Rabbi many continued to ply their father's trade as a means of making ends meet until they were old enough to take on students who would pay for their tutelage.

Somewhere along the line, Joseph died. This much is clear. Joseph, Mary's husband and Jesus' adopted father, is not mentioned in any of the texts after Jesus was twelve. So it is understood that he died sometime within the eighteen years between Jesus' teaching at the temple and the beginning of His ministry at the age of thirty. I can say this because several scriptures mention Jesus' siblings – brothers and sisters who were obviously younger than He was. So though we do not know when Joseph died, we know that he was in the picture for at least enough time to father siblings for Jesus. There is no record of Mary remarrying and it was clear that she was a widow at the time of Jesus' crucifixion because Jesus asked His disciple to look after her. Now we don't know the ages of Jesus' siblings, so we don't know for sure how much older than the others Jesus was but it is safe to assume that they weren't very far apart in age.

We know that Jesus was a Carpenter and most likely his brothers and father was as well. How successful their business was, we do not know. What we do know is that Nazareth was a small town so unless

Joseph took his boys to the neighboring towns that were more densely populated, like the Gentile city of Sepphoris, which was said to be only four miles from Nazareth and boasted a population of over twelve thousand people, it is safe to say their business wasn't very successful. After Joseph's death it is most likely that Jesus was thrust into a Patriarchal position, providing for the family until He was thirty years old – the age He would legally be able to begin His ministry according to Jewish Law.

Regardless of how it went, the point is that Jesus lived. He had a very active life prior to beginning His ministry. Jesus lived a normal life before He got baptized. From the waters of baptism, Jesus moved right out into the wilderness for forty days and forty nights, where He was tempted by Satan.

THE LIFE FAST

When Jesus returned from the wilderness, He wasn't the same. Now this isn't to say that the wilderness changed Him. I don't want to make it sound like not eating for forty days and going toe to toe with Satan somehow transformed Him. It didn't. However, something did change. The man that came out of the wilderness was a different man than the one that went in.

You see, Jesus prior to baptism was a family man. Whether He continued His Rabbinical training or went full-time into Carpentry after

Joseph passed, we do not know; it would be assumed, though, that He returned to His family to take over Joseph's responsibilities to the household. He took care of His mother as well as His siblings. Before He turned thirty years old, He was most likely the Father Figure in His home, making sure His sisters were treated respectfully by their suitors; making sure His brothers loved and cared for their wives or any women they may have been interested in. This all seems funny to me even as I write it because this is a side of Jesus that we don't often explore. Can you imagine what it must have been like to be a sibling of the King of Kings and Lord of Lords? Can you imagine the way He loved His family? Can you imagine how He spent time with each one individually, listening to them, encouraging them, teaching them? That must have been an amazing experience in and of itself.

Then one day Jesus went out to the river Jordan and was baptized by the wild man, John the Baptist – possibly His cousin. Jesus disappears for forty days and nights and when He returns, He is a man on a mission; a man who would spend the next three years marching towards His inevitable death while changing the world. What changed Him?

Matthew 3:16-17 (NIV)

16*As soon as Jesus was baptized, he went up out of the water. At that moment heaven was opened, and he saw the Spirit of God descending and alighting on him.* 17*And a voice from heaven said, "This is my Son, whom I love; with him I am well pleased."*

Jesus crossed a threshold, so to speak. He rose out of the waters of baptism and for the first time God acknowledged Him as His Son before men. From that moment, Jesus went on a fast. The scriptures say that the fast lasted forty days but that is only regarding his fast from food. I believe that Jesus embarked on a much longer fast and He fasted from more than just food. Romans 12:1, which is quoted in the beginning of this chapter, says that we must offer our bodies as a living sacrifice to God. After baptism, Jesus spent over a month fasting and praying, purging His body, preparing Himself for what was to come. When He returned He was about the mission. He was about His Father's business, not His own. He never returned to the person He was prior to baptism even though that person never sinned. So His not returning to that person is not to say that there was something wrong with who He was prior, it is to say that after baptism His focus had changed. The capstone of this transformation is in Matthew when someone approaches Jesus as He is teaching and says, *"Your mother and brothers are standing outside, wanting to speak to you."* Clearly something was going on that they felt required Jesus' immediate attention. This was Jesus' response:

Matthew 12:48-50 (NIV)

48He replied to him, "Who is my mother, and who are my
brothers?" 49Pointing to his disciples, he said, "Here are my mother and
my brothers. 50For whoever does the will of my Father in heaven is my
brother and sister and mother."

It seems kind of cold, doesn't it? Jesus did not all of a sudden decide to disown His family, although it sure can seem that way. He was simply fulfilling His calling. Remember, when Mary asked Jesus to turn the water to wine at the wedding celebration in Cana (John2:1-10), Jesus said *it was not yet His time.* Mary certainly understood what He meant by that – *there goes that word "yet" again* – it meant that there would come a time when He would reveal who He was to the world to the glory of the Father and at that time, things would change. When Jesus got baptized, that time had come. Even in the midst of it all He did not abandon His family. We know from scripture that at least one of His brothers was baptized into His name and even on the cross as His mother wept Jesus was concerned enough for her well-being that He appointed John to look after her (John 19:25-27). In no way did His dedication to the mission mean Jesus was turning His back on them; He was simply embracing the larger picture for His life that God apportioned to Him. He was no longer the head of just Joseph's family; He was stepping into His role as the head of God's family.

I Peter 2:21 (NIV)

21To this you were called, because Christ suffered for you, leaving you an example that you should follow in his steps.

Jesus went on a *Life Fast* and exemplified *true and proper worship for us.* He exemplified it not because He needed to but because He expects us to follow His example; He expects us to follow Him down that path – a *Life Fast* – a devotion or dedication that surpasses today's understanding of Christianity – true and proper worship as is fitting the God of all Creation.

Do you truly want to worship God in the proper fashion that He deserves and indicates in the scriptures? If you do then you can no longer claim Christianity from the pews. You can no longer claim Christianity on Saturdays or Sundays only. You can no longer claim Christianity only when it is convenient for you – in between cigarettes, fits of rage, use of obscenities, glimpses of pornography on the Internet and the like. It must become your life. *True worship is the transformation!* When you worship God there is no going back. To worship God in Truth is to Fast from who you were. You leave that person in the waters of baptism just as Jesus did and you live for God.

You are at your threshold. Christianity was never supposed to be a spectator's sport. You will either stay where you are and ignore your calling or you will cross on through to the other side; but you will do something.

THE THRESHOLD

Romans 12:1-2 (NIV)

1Therefore, I urge you, brothers and sisters, in view of God's
mercy, to offer your bodies as a living sacrifice, holy and pleasing to
God – this is your true and proper worship. 2Do not conform to the

pattern of this world, but be transformed by the renewing of your mind. Then you will be able to test and approve what God's will is – his good, pleasing and perfect will.

This is a promise from God. This is a conditional promise but a promise all the same. This promise requires action on your part; it requires that you do something. There are three things that are requirements in this passage and what's funny is that this isn't anything that Jesus hasn't said all along; it's just said a little differently, here.

1. You must facilitate the renewing of your mind. We must understand that it is not just our bodies that need to be trained but our minds as well. We must approach God with our minds in a malleable state, prepared and ready to be molded.
2. You must decide that you will no longer conform to the *(sinful)* pattern of this world. This is your decision and this requires action on your part. The onus is placed squarely on the individual to choose to no longer conform to the world. That means that this is possible for you. This is well within your capabilities.
3. You must offer your body as a living sacrifice to God. Once again the onus is on the individual. This is a choice; a choice that you have to make and carry out. You have to worship Him in Truth.

This is virtually the same thing that Jesus said in the past. We're going to take a look at that but before we do let's go a little deeper into what is being said here. The scripture says that we must no longer conform to the pattern of this world. I spoke about this in Chapter Eight in the section the Path of Transformation. I mentioned that true change occurs when faith confirmed becomes conviction and conviction creates greater faith, which once confirmed gives way to deep conviction and deep conviction gives way to a shift in the Mindset which creates the rewriting of our DNA; this – *the rewriting of the DNA* – is what leads to new behaviors that will become almost natural responses to whatever situation we are in. This cycle that occurs can become like a tornado funneling us upwards and closer to God. It *can* do this. Unfortunately, there can also be a downward spiral; a descent into deeper and darker sin as we reject God and His ways. When we commit ourselves to wickedness, the same sort of spiral is created as we venture deeper into sin and closer to destruction. This is the Pattern of this World spoken about in this scripture. So this *"tornado"* works in both directions, growing us towards God or towards destruction.

If we are caught up in the tornado but aimed in the direction of sin, the first thing we have to do is break the cycle. This is exactly what the scripture is talking about. We have to realize the path we are on and choose to no longer conform to the sinful patterns that threaten to destroy us. The scripture also says that we must offer our bodies as a living sacrifice to God for this is true and proper worship. This is about denial of self. You may have broken the cycle but without dealing with the desires inside of you that you have fed for years, you will return to those very same patterns of destruction. You have to face your demons! You have to deal with the desires of your heart and make them submit to Christ! This is a choice. This is not exactly easy but this is the cup that has been set before you. Just as Jesus in the Garden of Gethsemane prayed in Matthew 26:42, *"My Father, if it is not possible for this cup to be taken away unless I drink it, may your will be done"* you and I are looking down the mouth of a cup set before us, as well. Will you drink it? Will you allow God's Will to be done in your life? This is not an easy decision but then again it wasn't easy for Jesus, either. That is why this is the point where most fail. The fact that most fail at this point does not mean that this step should be skipped; this simply means that this step needs more attention and encouragement than the rest because this is the *back-breaker.* This is the point that breaks the will of most Christians but you need to stand firm. Drink the cup as Jesus did.

The next step the scripture mentions is allowing your mind to be renewed. This is done through beginning the new habits that will replace the old sinful ones. This is taking action towards getting the tornado of righteousness spiraling round and round as you grow towards God.

Luke 9:23 (NIV)

[23]Then he said to them all: "Whoever wants to be my disciple must deny themselves and take up their cross daily and follow me."

Do you see it? Jesus is saying the exact same thing that is said in Romans 12:1-2. It is a little more concise here but it is virtually the same thing. Denying yourself is to break the cycle of sin. Taking up your cross daily is to sacrifice yourself to God. Following Jesus is to create the new habits of righteousness that spiral you towards depth in your relationship with God. This is what the Jesus Mindset is all about.

NINETEEN:

"Reality is merely an illusion; albeit a very persistent one."

– Albert Einstein

A CONCEPT OF JESUS

WE KNOW ENOUGH FROM the scriptures to know Jesus' heart; we know enough to see the love He had for God and others but we don't actually *know Him*. The Bible says that there is so much more that He did and said that was not recorded than actually was recorded; so there are tons of miracles and lessons that we'll never hear. Now, we know enough from the scriptures to believe and have faith. God is real so He can touch our lives and turn our faithful steps to deep convictions and once we have the Holy Spirit inside of us, the sky should truly be the limit – He guides, protects and reveals deep things in the scriptures among other things. The bottom line is that we have an idea of who Jesus was; a pretty vivid image even but it is a lesser image still than that of the actual person. We have a concept of Jesus but Peter knew the man.

THE JESUS PETER KNEW

We know Jesus through the scriptures but we don't know Him like Peter did. We don't know Him as the disciples knew Him or even the people of His day. We don't relate to Him growing up as a child in a first century Jewish household, speaking Hebrew and Aramaic. We don't know what it was like to sit and laugh with Him; we don't know what it was like to hear His voice, see the intensity in His frame in His quieter moments or the softness in His eyes as He looked at the crowds with compassion. Peter did. Peter had a first-hand perspective of Christ. Peter did not follow a concept of Jesus; Peter followed Jesus!

I think this escapes us, sometimes. I think as we read the scriptures we inadvertently think that those around Jesus saw Him the same way we do, today – He is the Son of God; God in the flesh. That is simply not so. To those who lived and walked with Jesus, Jesus was a man – nothing more. How do you think knowing Jesus as a man and not the Son of God molded their mindset in those days? How does knowing Him as the Son of God and not as a man mold our mindset, today?

To Peter, Jesus was a man like any other so when Peter saw Jesus perform miracles what he saw was a man whom God was willing to work through because of the intensity of their relationship – His personal integrity and nearness to God. God worked through Him to perform wondrous signs. Peter saw a man doing these things and he was amazed at what God was willing to do through this mere man, a mere man like himself – not unlike you and me. When Jesus taught, Peter heard the words of a man that spoke the Words of God like none other before Him from the perspective of one who had a different relationship with God than anyone else.

The Jesus Peter knew was a man. According to scriptures, He wasn't even a handsome man (Isaiah 53:2). He was just a guy; a guy you could easily lose in a crowd but He was different because He exemplified the convictions He spoke of and resisted the urge to indulge in any kind of sin; He didn't even entertain the temptations that came. His every thought was pure. He loved people deeply. He saw in those around Him what they could not see in themselves. He inspired and uplifted. His words spoke to the heart. His actions challenged the soul. Even when He was hurting or weary He thought first of others; their needs, concerns and thoughts and He took it upon Himself to set their hearts and minds at ease or stir them up just enough to bring them to action. He was a local Rabbi who revealed truths that no one else revealed; saw in the scriptures things that no one else understood, things that made the so-called scholars question their beliefs. He was able to debate scripture with the best of them and spoke with an authority no one else dared to claim. For Peter, there were no New Testament Scriptures. All Peter and the other first century Christians had was the Old Testament. They didn't even have it in book form. According to Jewish Law every boy was taught from the age of five to memorize the entire Old Testament as it was read to them every day while they ate honey so that the association would be made in their minds between God's Word and the sweetness of honey. They were living what would become the New Testament. Peter walked with Jesus as He spoke the words that we read and quote in the scriptures. Peter didn't have the luxury of reading ahead to find out the outcome of whatever situation they found themselves in; he didn't know for certain that Jesus would rise from the dead. When Jesus hung on the cross, all that Peter knew for sure was that Jesus, like any other man, would die.

You see, the Jesus Peter knew was a man. So anything that Jesus did, Peter believed was possible for him, as well. The difference between himself and Jesus, he would have thought was simply the depth of Jesus' relationship with God, which means that if he were able to achieve the same depth of relationship, anything that was possible for Jesus would be possible for him. Now this is the catch: *Jesus encouraged him to believe this*. He didn't look at Jesus and say He was special; born of a certain lineage or anything like that – He was just Jesus; a Rabbi from Nazareth. We don't see Jesus that way, do we? We see Jesus as someone special. We see Him as *"otherworldly"* so to speak. He is the Son of God. He's not just a man. The problem with viewing Jesus this way is that it creates a division between us and Him that never existed for Peter and the other Disciples. They didn't see Jesus this way. Though He is the Son of God, we can tend to see Jesus this way and do so to a fault.

BELIEVING JESUS

They didn't follow a *Superhero Savior* who was above the frailties of Mankind – *temptations bounce off his chest like bullets to*

Superman – they followed Jesus . . . a man. As Peter followed Jesus, everything he saw Jesus do he wanted to do and Jesus encouraged him to do so. Peter didn't look at Jesus as an unattainable goal. Jesus was his friend. Jesus encouraged him daily and taught him how to overcome the world while in the flesh by simply choosing to do so. Peter got rebuked many times but he never got rebuked for having faith; he never got rebuked for living according to the precepts that Jesus taught him. Jesus believed in His disciples and His disciples *believed Him and believed in Him.* He expected them to do what He modeled for them. He expected this of them and because they saw Him as a man they came to expect the same of themselves. He expected them to do what He did. What would make us think that He expects any less, today? I believe that we often have a lesser expectancy for ourselves than that which Jesus has for us because we believe *in Him* but we often do not *believe Him.*

Why would Jesus encourage Peter to do something that was impossible? That makes absolutely no sense. Unless, of course, nothing was impossible for Jesus and He knew the same was true Peter – *for us* – but because of the limitations of our Perceived Realities, Jesus knew that we were shut off from Truth and He was simply trying to show them *Actual Reality.* According to the Jesus Mindset the word *Impossible* doesn't exist. So if Jesus encourages us to do something that means that He believes it is reality. If Jesus believes something is possible for us then it is possible; it is real, as real as real can be. To believe otherwise is to doubt God and ultimately to call Him a liar. What this means is, *what stands in the gap between what is and is not possible is simply whether you choose to believe Jesus, the scriptures and ultimately God.* Do you see that? If Jesus is the Truth and He says we can do something then what He just said is the Truth. Everything else is a lie. If Christ says we can do something then we can. To live in opposition to this Truth is to cling to the lies and patterns of this world and to call Jesus a liar. What we lack may be the will simply because we do not believe what He has said but we do not lack the ability. We need to understand that. It's easy to *believe in Jesus* because that doesn't require anything – *to believe Jesus* is something else entirely. There is a stark contrast between the two. *Believing in Jesus* is about believing *He is who He says he is.* In example, he is the Son of God; God in the flesh. *Believing Jesus* is about believing *you are who He says you are.* He says we are the Children of God, a Royal Priesthood, a Holy Nation belonging to God. Jesus calls us His brothers and sisters. This is vastly different because this demands that we change the way we think and what we think of ourselves. *The former demands that Jesus live up to who He is; the latter demands that we live up to who He says we are.* This demands that we drink the cup that is before us; this demands that we walk the walk. Are you living like the Spiritual Brother or Sister to Jesus that He says you are or are you sitting back basking in the fact that He lived up to who He is?

Peter believed Jesus and walked on water because of it. Jesus said he could and Peter trusted and believed Him then faithfully acted upon that belief. The fact that he lost faith and sank into the water is merely a speed bump along the path – what we need to pay attention to is not that he sank in the water but the fact that he walked on the water. Peter trusted what Jesus said, believed and applied faith – *he made no excuse for not living up to the calling* – and the impossible became possible. What is God waiting to do through you? What has not happened in your life because you have chosen to doubt rather than believe? You may have an idea of something that didn't happen or maybe you have accomplished a lot but you have no idea how much greater and further God could have taken you. You're still alive, though, aren't you? Don't get down about the past; get excited about the future. Remember that Caleb was eighty-five when he took the hill country of the Promised Land. There is no such thing as impossible; the future is always bright in the Lord, even if we are facing death! The victory is always ours.

John 11:4 (NIV)

4 *When he heard this, Jesus said, "This sickness will not end in death. No, it is for God's glory so that God's Son may be glorified through it."*

What impossible situation in your life is waiting on you? What situation in your life or someone else's has risen simply to bring glory to God through you? Trust in the Word of God – not just about what is written about Jesus and history but what is written about Mankind, what is written about us; what is written about you and me. Jesus didn't consider Himself special. He didn't see Himself as better than the rest of us. He saw us and continues to see us as His siblings; dearly loved siblings who have rebelled so long that we have forgotten who we are and the place we hold in God's heart. He shed His blood to make a way for us to come home but before He did that, He taught us how to live while in the flesh. That's the Jesus that Peter knew.

THE SUPERHERO SAVIOR

They say, *"Hindsight is 20/20"* and in the case of Jesus, truer words were never said. Today, we see Jesus in hindsight which is a very different view of Him than that of those who lived with Him and physically followed Him. We see the Son of God – God in the flesh; not necessarily a man. And who among us could really be like God, right?

Today it is very easy to see Jesus as a *Superhero Savior* who was more God than human and afforded every advantage imaginable to live a sin-free life. As slaves to sin in our own minds, it is near unfathomable to consider an average human being living and never once yielding to sin. Not once. Not even out of curiosity! The concept eludes us because left to ourselves, we are sinners; left to ourselves we are rebellious by choice. We don't just fall in to sin, we run to it with arms wide open! It's easier for us to believe that He had to have some kind of advantage because to believe that He simply chose not to sin is an outright condemnation of us and our choices. Perhaps He was enhanced like those comic book superheroes, genetically predisposed to righteousness. To us, living a sin-free life is equal to walking on the water – it's flat out impossible. We just can't relate. So to appease our egos, we create a concept of Jesus to follow that makes Him a little more palatable – we say that He was some kind of Superhero Savior but that isn't Jesus; that is just our concept of Him. We want Jesus to be some kind of Superhero because that is easier for us to accept but what we don't realize is that in doing this, we cheapen the sacrifice of Christ and open the door for excuses for offering God less than our best. I have come up with three excuses this kind of thinking creates: *the Clause Factor*; *the Insignificant Sacrifice* and *the Jesus of our own Choosing*; let's look at each one.

THE CLAUSE FACTOR

The Clause Factor is created when we say Jesus is the standard but because of our mentality towards Jesus, we make sure that God and everyone else knows that there is a clause built into *the Plan of Salvation* that God may not have been aware of – you see, *we're only human*! We're not perfect! *Jesus was a Superhero Savior. Therefore following His example is simply an unrealistic expectation. We should simply look upon Him with awe and wonder because we can never live up to His example. It's not that we don't want to follow Jesus; it's that we are incapable because we are "only human" and therefore inferior from inception.* In this vein of thinking, our humanity becomes our excuse. *I don't sin because I choose to; I sin because God made me inferior.* Ultimately, this kind of thinking blames God for our sin. This kind of thinking states, *"Well, He created me this way!"* I often find it funny when Christians get angry when a homosexual uses this argument for their sin not realizing that it is the Christian that used this excuse first. They're just jumping on the *bandwagon.*

Alexander Pope is credited for saying, *"To err is human, to forgive divine."* We accept it as Truth because everyone else in the world has but *is that True?* Did God create a faulty Human Being and place him in the Garden? If you look back at Genesis you will see that every time God created something He said it was *good* until after the creation of Man. After He created Adam and Eve, He said it was *very good.* We were made perfect. We are a *special* creation. That is why it is such a slap in the face when a Christian says that we evolved from animals. We are a separate creation; a greater creation. We are made by the same God so there will be similarities but we are not animals and never have been.

We were meant to rule the earth; God gave us dominion over all things (Gen. 1:28; Gen. 9:1-3). We were flawless but we were given free will and with that we chose to *become flawed.* To err is not human. God made us to be His Children. It is called *the Fall of Man* for a reason. *We became less when we sinned.* To err is not human; to err is to become sub-human; to err is to be *less* than a Man.

"I'm only human" has become an excuse for unrighteousness but *"I'm only human"* is a lie. The majority of Mankind is not human. You become Human when you are restored to Truth through the blood of Christ and choose to deny yourself, take up your cross and follow Him. Outside of that, humanity is a myth. As Christians, our humanity should be worn like a badge for all to see. We are Human because of Jesus; not for any other reason. We are human because we Love as we are Loved by God. This is why *Jesus is the way, the Truth and the life.* He lived according to the Will of God. That is the order of things. To live in any other manner is to oppose God's Will. When Jesus cursed the fig tree in Matthew 21 and it withered up and died that was not simply a display of power but a lesson about the order of things. If the tree does not fulfill its purpose it will be cut down. What does that say about you and me when we do not fulfill our purpose?

Matthew 5:13

13"You are the salt of the earth. But if the salt loses its saltiness, how can it be made salty again? It is no longer good for anything, except to be thrown out and trampled underfoot."

One of the reasons hypocrisy is rampant in the church is because of this clause. Too many Christians view their humanity as a fault and Jesus' example as an unattainable goal. Too many of us would never speak these words but when you say you are *"only human"* what you are actually saying is that Jesus is an arrogant, Superhero Savior who was afforded every advantage to live sin-free yet holds us to an impossible standard. Is that what you believe and have faith in? If you believe you are *"only human"* and that is somehow an excuse or a reason for your sin then that is exactly what you are saying with every decision you make. Please don't make that decision. Let us toss this excuse from our minds, hearts and psyche and cling to a God that can and already has made the impossible possible.

THE INSIGNIFICANT SACRIFICE

The Insignificant Sacrifice is when we look to the heavens or to each other and say, *"If Jesus was God then so what if He died on the cross or lived a sinless life? He was God! What's the big deal?"* The Insignificant Sacrifice and The Clause go down a similar path. Where the two veer off from one another is the focus of the complaint. Where the Clause looks at Jesus' example as being unattainable, the Insignificant Sacrifice looks at the sacrifice, itself. This kind of thinking downplays every aspect of Jesus' suffering because, well . . . He was God. So what if He didn't hurl insults back at those who spat upon Him. So what if He refused the gall. So what if nails were driven into His wrists or legs, couldn't God simply turn off the pain and whistle through it? What's the big deal that He was sinless? I mean, really. It's not like He was going to sentence Himself to Hell if He did, anyways, right? I've actually had someone ask this during a Bible Study. What this vein of thought is attempting to establish is that Jesus lived by a different set of rules. He actually did, if you really think about it but that is because of our doing not His. Sin is our denial of the Truth and our choosing to not live according to God's Will but our own – a different set of rules. Jesus came to reacquaint us with who we have always been; Jesus came to reacquaint us with Truth – with Love. That is not what this excuse is trying to establish, though. What this excuse attempts to suggest is that there really were no stakes involved for Jesus because He was God. He can't relate to us! He doesn't know what it's like to *really* suffer. In this sense, Jesus becomes like the child of a billionaire who is afforded every advantage in life and once he is successful looks at the poor child or even the middle class child and wonders why can't he or she pull themselves up by their bootstraps like he did? The poor or middle class child looks back at the billionaire child and scoffs, *"Like you know what it's like to suffer or to work hard; to struggle! You got by on your father's money and if not his money, his name! You are not successful because of you; you are successful because of who your father is."*

Do you see how destructive this kind of thinking can become for the Christian? This person can completely negate the cross in his life because he sees a Jesus that was more Superhero than human being. And before you say no Christian would say that. Take note that the person who said those words to me was someone who said he was a Christian and claimed to have been one for quite some time. You'll be surprised what some people believe when you begin to get in there with them and start having deeper conversations.

THE JESUS OF OUR CHOOSING

Just like the other two, this version of the Superhero Savior excuse breaks away a little further down the path. While the other two questions Jesus' example and sacrifice, respectively; this one rejects Jesus altogether.

You might be wondering how someone can reject Jesus yet call themselves a Christian. Actually, it's not as far-fetched as one might think. Israel did it. Before Saul was chosen as Israel's first King, Israel had God for their King and as the scriptures say, eventually the people of Israel requested a human King in His stead (1 Sam. 8). The people of Israel wanted to be like all the other nations and have someone – *a man* – to place on a pedestal; someone they could relate to and identify with. It's almost like they wanted to save God for the Sabbath and have a King to laud praises on the rest of the week. They wanted a man in God's seat and we often do the same thing, whether that man is ourselves or someone else. We often tell ourselves that Jesus can't relate to us when actually it is not Jesus that cannot relate to us but we who do not wish to relate to Him. Those who subscribe to this mentality usually don't want to be *sinless* they simply want to sin *less*. They want to hold onto the sin they want to hold onto without any outside interference. They don't want an almighty, perfect God looking over their shoulder; they want a man who is as flawed as they are holding them accountable because that way, they don't feel as bad about their sin. They don't want to follow God; they want to follow a flawed man whom they can accuse should he ever overstep his boundaries and speak to them about their sin.

No one was more *human* than Jesus. Adam gave in to sin. Adam was no more created to sin than Jesus was but he yielded to the temptation while Jesus resisted the devil. Adam was God's first Son and like the story of the Prodigal Son in Luke 15, he ran off with his inheritance and defiled himself. Jesus simply did not. Adam strayed; Jesus was faithful. Mankind was not created to sin but we have chosen to follow the pattern of this world; the pattern etched out by Adam's erroneous behavior – *erroneous behavior that all of Adam's descendants suffer from – we reject God for a human King*. To this day, we continue to suffer because of this mentality that says we can do it all of our own accord. We don't want to *need* God and if we finally break down and admit that we do, we want to do it on our terms. Those who cling to this excuse will consider Jesus great but His example is too lofty – no one can ever attain that. Thus these people reject Christ's example for the example of someone else – a grandparent, a minister or father figure of some sort; a figurehead to take God's place in their lives. The problem with this is of course the placing of a man in the seat of God in the individual's life. When that human falls – *and he will most certainly fall* – the individual who placed him there scorns both the man that failed as well as God as though he was told to worship the man rather than our Father in Heaven.

I remember in the late 1980s, following the Televangelist scandals; there was this huge fallout in Christendom. One was caught with prostitutes while another said God threatened to kill him if he could not raise thirty million dollars in thirty days. Many threw their hands up in the air and walked away from their professed faith, completely disillusioned by Christianity. Men sinned and lied and people acted as though the world was coming to an end. The thing is the Bible never mentioned that any of these TV ministers was the Savior of Man. They were men; just like any other. Admonish them, if you must, but don't walk away from God. My fellowship of churches went through something similar to this in the early 2000's. A few church leaders sinned and it became this huge thing – many walked away from God. How does that even begin to make sense? Someone sins and somehow that reflects poorly on God? It really makes no sense. No one walks away from God because of someone else's sin; if you choose to walk away from God it is simply because you were looking for a way out. We were not called to follow men; we were called to follow God!

THE ZOMBIE APOCALYPSE

For three years Jesus hunkered down with the twelve and imparted His Mindset upon them; His thoughts, attitudes and expectations. He expected them to adopt His mindset and allow it to become their own; allow His Mindset to become their convictions. You see Jesus wasn't just about miracles and healing the sick or feeding and teaching the masses. He wasn't even just about dying on the cross. As much as He was about all of those things, Jesus was also about imparting His heart and His Mindset upon a few, knowing that those few would go out with His heart and mindset and impart the same upon others. In doing so, just a handful of men could turn the world upside down in a single generation – and they did!

Research shows – *and it's hard to believe that someone seriously spent time and money researching this, but it serves my purpose at the moment, so I won't complain* – that if a true zombie pandemic occurred where one infected person bites another, thus infecting that person and creating a fellow zombie, at our current global population of a little over seven billion people, our entire planet would be overrun with zombies inside a month. Without this research, Jesus figured out that the easiest way to start a movement that would span the globe in a single generation was to focus not on the entire world but a handful of people. Christianity was never about filling pews in buildings on Saturday or Sunday mornings. Jesus wasn't interested in creating more Pharisees, Sadducees and all the other ruling factions of ancient Israel. Jesus was about creating twelve carbon copies of Himself that would each go out and do as He did – go out and create carbon copies of Jesus. One could say that Jesus understood the mathematics and logistics involved. He didn't take it upon His shoulders to convert the entire known world; He didn't even go after the Samaritans or the Gentile. He didn't put that kind of pressure on His disciples, either. Jesus was smart enough to understand that converting the world in one fell swoop was not the way to go. He knew exactly what He was doing. Though He spoke to large crowds, at times, He also turned away many. Those Sermon on the Mount moments were more or less highlights. Instead, Jesus focused the majority of His energy on a few, close quarter relationships and poured Himself into each individual leaving an example for us to follow – small groups focused on instilling the heart of Christ and loving each other enough to hold one another accountable. The way for salvation was paved with His blood but the plan to reach the world was a joint effort that every Christian is to take part in. This method did not change. So it is still an expectation that every Christian is to become a carbon copy of Jesus and to find others to have those close quarter relationships with to pour not themselves, but Jesus into.

TWENTY:

"Happiness and freedom begin with a clear understanding of one principle: some things are within your control and some things are not."

– Epictetus

GOD'S REALITY

THERE IS THIS OLD joke about a man who falls off of a cliff and manages to grab onto a root sticking out of the side of the mountain. Below him is certain death and there is no one above to help him. He screams and cries out for help as he feels his hold slipping. Finally the man in desperation calls out to God and God answers. The man asks God to save him and God tells him if he wants to be saved, he must let go of the root. There is a long pause and then the man calls out in a loud voice again, *"Is anyone else up there?"*

If you haven't heard it a dozen times already, the joke is enough to put a smile on the face but there is a very real concept portrayed here. If God's reality is *Actual Reality* than that means that we have lived our lives thus far trying to maintain the lie of our Perceived Realities rather than trying to take hold of the Truth that Jesus has been trying to show us all along. In Actual Reality, we are all the individual hanging from the cliff and that root we're clutching to is our Perceived Reality. Jesus is yelling to us to let go and trust His understanding for our lives because Truth is only found in Him. We look down and around and all we see are the lies of our Perceived Realities and the sway they desire to have over us and rather than let go, we tend to hang on tighter. Like Peter as he walked on the water, the lies of his Perceived Reality eventually choked out the faith until he began to sink back into the lies that possessed him before. We hold on to our Perceived Realities for dear life, struggling against God, completely missing the point: *His reality lies outside of the reach of our reality because our reality isn't real – it has never been real and never will be. What we call reality is a lie! Actual Reality – God's Reality – is what lies beyond the limitations we have adopted and/or created for ourselves.*

When Jesus walked on the water He was doing the impossible right before the eyes of His disciples. He was broadening their sense of what can and cannot be done in the flesh. He was offering them Truth or more accurately, He was smashing their ceilings and exposing them to the vastness of space. You see, the only reason we consider what Jesus did *"the Impossible"* is because we are still mentally enslaved within our Perceived Realities. In Actual Reality, in Jesus' reality – *the Jesus Mindset* – all things are possible through the Father. There is no such thing as impossible. *Impossible* does not exist.

When Jesus walked on the water, He gave Peter a glimpse of *His Reality* and when Peter asked to walk on the water, what he was really asking was to not just glimpse Jesus' Reality but to *experience it.* Peter's mind was opened. He was there – basking in the glory of the mindset of Christ; God's Reality. For a moment he walked and experienced Truth. He experienced the freedom that can only come through the blood of Christ. I would think He loved it but his Perceived Reality was persistently knocking on the side of his head trying to draw him back into the warmth and coziness of the lies that have been with him since birth. Actual Reality slipped through his fingers as the lies came crashing back on top of him and he began to sink in the water.

Do you remember what it was that Jesus said to Peter? Jesus asked, *"Why did you doubt?"*

WHY DID YOU DOUBT?

Here's something to think about: *if Jesus asked Peter 'why did you doubt', whose faith enabled Peter to walk on the water?* Most people assume incorrectly that Jesus allowed Peter to walk on the water. If Jesus allowed Peter to walk on the water, he'd still be walking right now! He would have never sunk in the water if Peter walked because of Jesus. Peter didn't walk on water according to Jesus' faith; he walked according to *his faith.*

Jesus exemplified a level of wisdom and understanding that surpassed that of all who witnessed this miracle. By doing so, He opened up Peter's mind to the possibility; to the Truth. In essence Jesus walking on the water gave Peter permission to believe beyond his own understanding and he believed but it didn't end there. When Jesus called him out on the water Jesus gave Peter the opportunity and the permission to turn that belief to faith and for a moment, he did. It did not solidify into conviction because Peter's faith wavered. Doubt and fear eventually crept in and Peter sank into the water but for a brief moment Peter glimpsed Truth. Peter had not yet bought into the Jesus Mindset and so he only took a few steps. He eventually rejected the Truth for the lies he was all too familiar with. Peter wasn't ready at that moment to walk in the Jesus Mindset but a time would soon come when he would. He didn't realize then that every faulty step he took was in preparation for the leaps and bounds to come. One day Peter would let go of the root and he would never be the same.

BUBBLES

I believe every single one of us are living in bubbles constructed of our own limited understanding, fears and limitations and we call this bubble *reality*. It is actually our own Perceived Reality. The Truth is there is nothing real about these self-imposed prisons. They exist only in our minds and are designed to keep our minds sedated and blind so that we never come to know the Truth. Our realities are lies we have constructed and chosen to accept as truth. Like the child hiding under a blanket and believing the rest of the world has faded away, mankind has encased himself within bubbles that shield us from the Truth and trap us within our own lies. All God is trying to do is open our hearts and minds to the Truth so that we can burst these bubbles and be set free from our own Perceived Realities to explore the unlimited possibilities of His. Like the joke that started this chapter, once we let go of our Perceived Reality – *once the bubble is popped with a pin* – the only place we can possibly fall is into *His Reality*. It would truly be like coming out of the Matrix but instead of returning to a world of desolation we would be opened up to a reality with endless possibilities – the realization that all things are and always have been possible with God; nothing is beyond His ability. This realization can be earth-shattering if and when we truly grasp it, understand it, accept it, believe it and put it into practice. This Truth shatters our old way of thinking and opens our hearts and minds to a new way – *the Way, the Truth and the Life; the Jesus Mindset!*

Everything that you've read so far was to bring you to this point. You are at your threshold. It is time for you to cross on through to the other side.

I am going to say something that I did not say before and I believe it needs to be said. The Jesus Mindset is not a destination. The Jesus Mindset is *the threshold*. Once you cross through, the sky is truly the limit. The depth of relationship that you and God acquire is determined by your level of surrender. God wants all of you. How deep are you willing to go with Him? Dig deep; dig deeper every day. Dig deeper than you've ever imagined. Once you've surrendered you will find it is no longer about you but about what God can do through you. Surrender all and be amazed. In a world of selfishness, true freedom is found in being entirely selfless. Let go of the root; let go of the excuses; let go of your false reality – just let go . . . and sin no more!

The Beginning . . .

A portion of the proceeds from this book will be donated to HOPE worldwide to further their efforts to bring hope to others and change lives.

Bringing hope. Changing lives

HOPE worldwide serves the poor from Haiti to Jamaica, Russia to South Africa, China to the Middle East as well as Europe, Great Britain and the United States. They provide homes for orphans and leprosy patients, care for the sick, educate the disadvantaged and meet the needs of children and seniors around the globe. This is accomplished through various outreach venues including but not limited to: AIDS/HIV treatment and prevention in South Africa; Malalai Emergency Maternity Ward in Afghanistan; Disaster response efforts in Asia, Africa, North America and the Caribbean; Elder care in Eastern Europe and the Sihanouk Hospital Center of HOPE in Cambodia.

For more information about HOPE worldwide or to make a donation, visit the website: www.hopeww.org

HOPE worldwide has a High Value Charity rating. 87% of expenditures go directly to program costs.

Our support of HOPE worldwide does not, in any way, reflect any endorsement, on their part, of this book or any content therein.

A portion of the proceeds from this book will be donated to the Sturge-Weber Foundation to continue their efforts in their mission to educate the public, empower and support families and friends of those with Sturge-Weber Syndrome, Port Wine Birthmarks and Klippel-Trenaunay Syndrome, as well as fund research for these conditions.

The Sturge-Weber Foundation

The Stronger the Wind, the Tougher the Trees.

For more information on the Sturge-Weber Foundation, information about Sturge-Weber Syndrome, Port Wine Birthmarks & Klippel-Trenaunay Syndrome or to make a donation, please visit the website: www.sturge-weber.org

The Sturge-Weber Foundation is a 501(c) (3) non-profit organization supported by individual and corporate gifts and grants. All donations are tax deductible.

Our support of the Sturge-Weber Foundation does not, in any way, reflect any endorsement, on their part, of this book or any content therein.

About the Author:

Christian Transformational Coach and Author, Richard Binns, has spent the last twenty-six years serving churches in New York City and the Greater Hartford area in Connecticut. He and his wife, Yasmin have been married for over twenty-three years and have three wonderful children: Magnus-Storm, Summer-Sky and Anniston-Earl.

Made in the USA
Coppell, TX
22 April 2022

76914435R00146